Clarence A. Webster

Hawaii

A Snap Shot

Clarence A. Webster

Hawaii
A Snap Shot

ISBN/EAN: 9783337148331

Printed in Europe, USA, Canada, Australia, Japan

Cover: Foto ©Andreas Hilbeck / pixelio.de

More available books at **www.hansebooks.com**

Hawaii...

.. A Snap Shot

❀

BEING THE RECORD OF A TRIP

TO THE

"PARADISE OF THE PACIFIC"

IN WHICH THE TRUTH OF GENERAL IMPRESSIONS MORE THAN LITERAL—
AND OFTEN MISLEADING—FACT IS OFFERED . . . .

BY

CONFLAGRATION JONES

ILLUSTRATED BY
ART YOUNG AND OTHERS

CHICAGO:
SMITH & COLBERT
1893.

A Word Before Starting.

IN these doubtful days there are a lot of vital and pertinent questions asked about the Hawaiian Islands, the people and their ways, which the encyclopedia and the last Hawaiian census report fail to answer. Do not think I would question the value of encyclopedias or other four-pound books. By students and thoughtful people everywhere they have been found matchless for pressing creases in trousers and doubtless have other uses; but they do not cover the entire field. The following work tells all which the encyclopedia, through thoughtlessness, inadvertance or pressure on its columns failed to mention.

There are some things truer than fact,—concrete fact without its proper explanitory background is often misleading. It has been the aim of the writer not so much to marshal facts in line as to present a picture, the verity of the impression of which, although necessarily superficial, cannot be seriously questioned. Not that there are not facts enough in the work to satisfy the most radical Gadgrind, but the intent has been to disguise their taste.

The observations upon which the work was based were made just prior to the downfall of the monarchy; but the conditions of life were and can be in no way changed by any political upheaval, past or prospective.

CONFLAGRATION JONES.

CHICAGO, November, 1893.

THE HAWAIIAN ISLANDS AND THE REST OF THE WORLD.

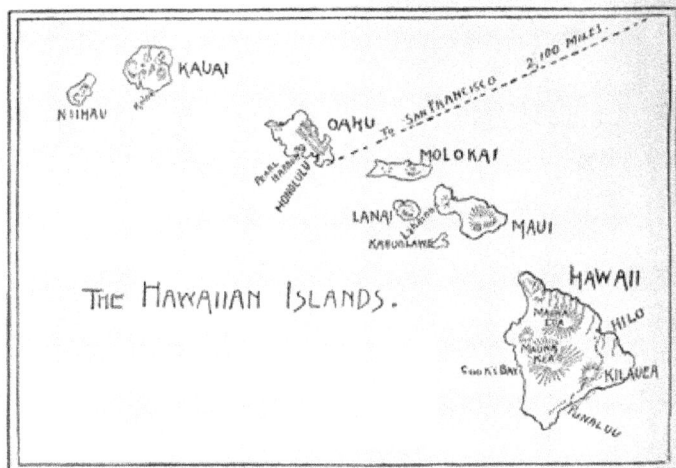

THE HAWAIIAN ISLANDS.

First View of the Islands.

CHAPTER I.

Remarks on the Water—The Pacific Ocean Nothing but a Large,
Damp Confidence Game—Sea-Sickness and Its Remedies—
Life on Shipboard.

PEAKING of waves reminds me that we traveled over the picturesque Salt Water route via Seasickville, giving us a good view of Heaveup Junction and the fine rural spot of Bile-on-the-Billow. It is an even seven days' trip from San Francisco to Honolulu over the bluest water that a washwoman ever used to rinse her clothes. I know the water is blue because I spent hours every day hanging over the rail in deep contemplation, and for other purposes not worth mentioning.

The distance traversed is supposed to be 2,100 miles, but the Oceanic Steamship Company had a generous streak on and gave us action for fares. I have carefully estimated the lurches to port—at the rate of two per minute—to be 20,160 in number, and the lurches to starboard would, of course, be the same in number. That would give us something like 4,000 miles of movement. This, they inform me, was not the regular thing, but was gotten up for our especial delectation.

I was told at home by an English ex-naval officer

Mr. Balboa Christening the Pacific.

that the Pacific was always like a billiard-table in the full bloom of health. I don't believe he ever saw the Pacific. I think he got his information out of the primary geography that I worried through under pressure in the days of my childhood. According to the book, the ocean was named the Pacific—"the peaceful"—by a mendacious Greaser called Balboa, who is portrayed as standing on a bluff in the attitude of a political speaker waiting for the applause to subside. The ocean is before him. His arm is extended like that of a man trying to flag a waiter whom he has failed to tip. His other arm and the rest of his person is in the posture of deep meditation. He is trying to think out a name which will enhance the price of Honolulu real estate and stimulate the Samoan boom.

I have a disposition like a child; I am not revengeful, but I would like to meet this man Balboa in some place where I had plenty of friends to drag us apart and hold me back, and prevent me reddening my hands in the gore of a fellow man. I would like to tell him in some neat but rich and juicy sarcasm how there is a position yawning for him as circulation affidavit editor of a daily paper.

I was led to believe that my middle name was Jonah, and that it was all my fault, as usual. The chief officer of the Australia, the ship which ferried us over to the islands, insisted that the weather was exceptional, and that we should have made the previous run, or, failing in that, the one following, when, as he predicted, the sea would be as flat as a tennis court.

To be urged to wait for the next boat, and to take passage in the same under an alias, after being a day and a half on a route that can't even boast of a milk station or a wood siding—or anything else that would give a repentent sinner a show to turn back—this was the kind of thing to make a man distrust friendly advice for the rest of his natural life. It was offered, too, at a time when I had sent my stomach down to the ship's laundry to have some stiffening starch put in. I was sick—both sea-sick and sick of the sea.

The Only Sick Man on Board.

Other people had "touches of malaria," and all that sort of thing.

I am the only person of my acquaintance who had common, every-day sea-sickness. The first two or three days out the ship's physician did a rushing business in the consolation line.

A ship's doctor draws a comfortable salary for explaining to cabin passengers how it is not sea-sickness which has snowed them under, but something mysterious with a long Latin name which sounds like a verse in the Polish declaration of independence.

You understand that the rules of a ship forbid

Interested in Flying Fish.

profanity forward of the gangways, and it is mighty comforting to sea-sick passengers to lie in their bunks and have an accomplished linguist sit by and call their malady hard names and sass it in a dead language.

Burridge, my *companion du voyage*, as they say in the south of Ireland, came on deck with a new disease every morning. When he bobbed up the first day I thought he was wearing a dough mask. He looked wildly around and commenced to make motions with his mouth like a district schoolboy who is out to speak a declamation, and the wrong lines keep rising to the surface and have to be swallowed with great effort.

"Sea-sick, old man?"

"I? I sea-sick? Not much, but I'm not feeling well. The doctor says I've got a touch of information of the spaghetti. I tell you they've got a mighty able physician on board. He can tell what ails you without asking a question. He said I had been eating something. Excuse me a moment—they say that flying fish can be seen. I'm very much interested in flying fish," and then he shot off looking for a secluded nook out of sight of the ladies, where he could give his "information" a fair field and no favor.

Everyone has a pet cure for sea-sickness, and Burridge has a new one. He lay moaning in his berth, crying out for something to stay down. "I wonder if glue would stick?" he said. It was but an idle fancy on which he had no thought of realizing, but it furnished me with an idea. I rang for the berth steward, who was a solemn personage, said "sir" with painful frequency, and grudgingly gave up sympathy in a purely official way about his watch.

"Please bring that poor, sick gentlemen in No. 33 some liquid glue," I ordered.

"Yes, sir. Spalding's or LePage's, sir?"

"LePage's, and fix it up with salt and pepper so that it will be tempting to the palate—and, by the way, call it extract of beef."

"Yes, sir; glue, sir, with salt and pepper, sir," and

Exercise After Meals.

the steward inserted his thumb in his right ear and jerked it away again in a wax figuresque way.

I departed, not to interfere with the onward progress of events. In an hour or two Burridge came on deck with the fixed celluloid smile of a premiere dansu-

ese. "That extract of beef is just what I needed. It's the only thing that will associate with me long enough to get acquainted. It's immense."

"My boy, that wasn't extract of beef. That was glue."

He became ghastly as the idea struck in. "Good heavens, I am lost! My insides are stuck together and I will never eat again. I knew this foreign travel would be the death of me." A brutal sailor, noticing his emotion, came up, touched his hat, and requested him to "Please go leeward and weep in the sea, if it is all the same to you."

The Pacific Ocean is a perfect paradise for that class of people who are inquisitive about their neighbors and who do not feel easy in their minds unless they know what their acquaintances had for dinner. I have always endeavored to keep dark what I have been eating, particularly after partaking of onions, but on Senor Balboa's Pacific it was of no use. The fatal secret was wrested from me three times per day, and the gossip mongers had it all their own way.

I must say that the officers of the Australia were very considerate. Whenever a passenger came on deck and looked like a chicken in the act of drinking, they invariably turned their faces and affected to see a ship in great distress on the horizon. The tourists were thus allowed to seek vacant spots on the rail and sing solos to the old and well-known words, which commenced "Yeep—Yeep—oho—waugh—good heavens Yeep." It sounded like a Kanaka love song, but it wasn't. On the Atlantic the officers use a cold British stare or an official smile on the victim which, added to the remorse of a guilty stomach, makes the tourist pant for a Pullman car.

Diamond Head, Honolulu.

CHAPTER II.

Mutiny by the Smart Alexander of the Ship—Our Welcome to
Honolulu—Surprises—A Chinese Hotel Clerk.

WE HAD a mutiny on
the ship. The mutineer was a young man
from Chicago whose
entire working capital
consisted of a male
parent who cashed
sight drafts with the
reckless abandon of infatuation, and nerve that a diamond couldn't scratch. He said that his father sent
him to take a trip on salt water and advised him to
indulge in ocean bathing.

I always had a suspicion that the old gentleman
wanted him to get on terms of familiar intimacy with
the salt, salt sea, in the hope that the saline matter
would strike in.

This young man—I will call him De Pett—started
in by giving all of us advice like a dollar fortune-teller.
He tackled a banker and told him about the mistakes
he had made in his youth, and advised him to reform
and go fishing whenever old Financial Crash struck
town.

De Pett even reached for me. I was traveling
about one-half or two-thirds in cog. He sidled up to
me with the idea of seeing me about it. I quickly
made up my mind to feign insanity if he should commence to exude advice. However, he merely asked,
"What's your line, Mister?"

Now the only line I have in the world is a clothes
line in my back yard, and Mrs. Jones is president of it
at that. "You mean my business?" I asked.

"Yes; what's your business out here?"

"I am here to introduce to the benighted savages
of the South Seas the Jones perforator and embosser."

"What's that for, may I ask?"

"The Hawaians, you understand, have been eating
their tripe plain. I will introduce my machine which
embosses and perforates tripe, as it is eaten in the most
refined Michigan avenue circles."

I supposed that his appetite for conversation
would be cloyed, but I was mistaken. He chipped
right in with: "Well, if your tripe embosser is a failure I should advise you to put ink on the teeth of the
machine and sell it to the natives for tatooing themselves. I think that would work nicely."

I saw at once that I would have to offer extra inducements to get him to shun me. I don't want to say
too much of the young man's doings, but he was one
of the most perfect specimens of the smart Alexander
in existence, and all he needed was chloroform and a
railroad spike driven through his wishbone impaling
him to the bottom of a glass case to be of the utmost
value to science.

The signs notifying the passengers of the laws of

8

the ship aggravated him worse than parliamentary rules do a woman's rights convention. There was one notice which read :

> PLEASE DONT' JOSH THE MAN
> AT THE WHEEL.

and another which remarked :

> PASSENGERS ARE REQUESTED NOT TO BOR-
> ROW TOBACCO OF OFFICERS OF THE
> WATCH.

De Pett looked at them in frowning indignation.

He Would Sue the Captain.

" I'm from Chicago, and the Constitution of the United States accords me the right to josh any one I please."

Then he went up and tried it. Captain Hou-dlette called his attention to the literature on the sign-boards in the quiet way of sea captains.

De Pett turned on him in a blaze of magnificent wrath. " I want you to understand that I am a gen-tleman, and no ordinary tourist," which he wasn't. " I have paid the Oceanic Company $125 for a round-trip passage, and I'm going to have $125 worth of kind and gentlemanly treatment, sir. I demand the full amount, with no discount for cases, exchange or cart-age, sir, or I will sue the company. I will report you, sir. Yesterday the ship was rocking severely, sir, and I wanted to walk on deck. I asked you on behalf of myself and some lady friends on board to anchor the boat an hour or two so that it would stand still and we could take our exercise. You refused, sir. You merely said, ' Holy Sailor, anchor in five miles of water ?' That

answer was very offensive to a gentleman, and I will not sit quiet under it."

One of his acquaintances dragged the young man away and told him he was guilty of mutiny, and mutiny was usually the thing which superinduced wind failure through suspension at the yardarm by a coarse, vulger rope. If he didn't look out he would finish the voyage in irons anyway.

De Pett subsided with a swoon and kept pretty dark after that, avoiding the Captain, cutting the latter off from his most reliable source of amusement. But De Pett kicked behind his back, and said he thought the skipper was sojering. He hadn't seen him pull a rope or cuss out the men since he started, and he didn't holler his orders like they do on the canals at home

De Pett thought he wasn't the kind of man to stand at the bow when we got into the region of ice-bergs and shove 'em out of the way with a pitchfork. He wanted the boat run like a Blue Island avenue horse car.

When, one morning a short time afterward, a ribald sign stating :

> PASSENGERS MUST NOT FEED PEA-
> NUTS TO THE CAPTAIN

was found tacked to that dignitary's door, every one looked at De Pett, who strove to look as unconscious of guilt as a man who just discovers he has drank from a finger bowl, thinking he was getting an extra large glass of lemonade.

Early on the morning of the seventh day word

Official Tongue Inspection.

was passed forward that we could unlash our livers preparatory to going ashore, the rest of the trip being under the lea of Oahu, the island on which Honolulu is located, and therefore free from the deadly Pacific roll which we always had for breakfast with our coffee.

The only thing I could find fault with was the way

we sighted land. No one yelled "Land ho!" I expected to see one of the hired men go up to the six-
teenth story of the rigging and make that cheering remark, just as it is portrayed on the plug tobacco advertisements. I will never put any faith in plug tobacco
after this. They told me they discontinued the practice after sending up a sailor from Boston, who called
down:

"Land agricultural implement!"

Upon going on deck we found the mountains
2,000 or 3,000 feet high, sticking out of the water on
the starboard bow, while off to the south loomed the
faint outline of Molokai, the island on which the lepers
are sequestered.

Welcome to Honolulu.

The first glance at Oahu has been described as forbidding and bare, and as though a quartz crusher
would be required to make soil out of it. It was yel-
lowish brown and gray in the morning sun and looked
to me like a lot of cooking-school cakes that had erupted
when half baked.

There was, however, a bright fringe of verdure
along the coast line, with an occasional cocoanut palm
sticking up like a feather duster with two-thirds of its
tail-feathers jerked out.

I was informed that the mountains were once covered with verdure, but that the wild goats had eaten
them bare. The poor goats of Honolulu had but few
bill boards to feed on, and were forced by dire necessity
to fall back on just common leaves and grass. The
islands ought to encourage theatrical enterprises which
are lavish with three-sheet posters and save its foliage.

Rounding Diamond Head, a volcanic promontory
about five miles from Honolulu, that city bursts upon

the view. There is much of greenery and much to re-
mind a man, besides the temperature, that he is in the
tropics.

The town lies on a gentle slope a few miles in
width, having a background of mountains, whose sum-
mits are almost always enshrouded in clouds and mist.

Honolulu does a large and growing business in
the port line, with all the modern conveniences—quar-
antine officers empowered by law to make people stick
out their tongues, custom house officers who write
Chinese passwords on your luggage in chalk, pilots who
come out with plug hats with election news, and all
that. The town, it must be remembered, has a population of over 25,000, and the arrival of the steamer is
the only circus it has.

Our reception was very flattering. As the Australia was warped up to the dock we saw that they
were all there to receive us. I said all—I mean all but
two. One of the two had broken his leg the day before and sent his regrets. The other was dead, and I
think deserved to be excused on that account.

But the balance of the populous, who had been
notified at daylight by telephone from the opposite side
of the island when the steamer was sighted, flocked
around so that we did not notice the fact that there
were two absentees.

The sight was gay beyond the powers of description—that is to say, of any one but a society editor.
The galaxy of Hawaiian beauty was something to make
the timbers of the dock creak.

Hundreds of coy Kanaka belles, none of them
weighing less than 250 pounds, and clad in bright-hued
Mother Hubbards, stood there waving their handkerchiefs, entranced at the spectacle of Burridge, who stood
well up forward in an elaborate toilet, with his hand
over his heart, as though he were playing an engage-
ment in the Eden Musee as Emperor William in wax.

A citizen of Honolulu whom I had up to that moment regarded as a friend said to us: "This is a fine
reception they are tendering you, and you ought to get
up and thank them for it. I assure you it is the custom of the country, and the people will feel hurt if you
fail to respond."

Burridge said he couldn't make a speech except
when he was mad, and so the duty fell upon me.

I leaped to the rail and commenced: "Ladies
and—and gentlemen of Honolulu-lulu-lu: In behalf
of Mr. Burridge and myself I wish to thank you for
this magnificent demonstration. When I look upon
this vast throng I feel overpowered, as it were, over-
whelmed——" Just then a low, vulgar sailor pitched
quoits with a coil of rope, using my lithe frame for a
peg. He scored a ringer the first time.

I sank to the deck and the thousands of gazelle-
eyed native beauties screamed with mocking laughter,
while my friends unwound about twenty fathoms of
rope off my anatomy. I have my suspicion that the
Honolulu man knew all the time that the crowd wasn't
there to see us, and if he was trying to joke with me I
don't think it was a bit funny.

Honolulu was quite a shock to people of our delicate nerves. I once heard a dime museum lecturer, in
exhibiting the tatooed man, say that he was a native

of the Sandwich Islands, and somehow I got the idea that the prominent citizens of that city went around with the latest style of winter trousers, consisting largely of red and blue ink in designs of eagles, scrolls,

"Climb a Cocoanut Palm for Dessert."

the American flag, and reptiles all embroidered on the cuticle in a way calculated to last.

When I discovered my error it was a great disappointment, for I expected that the city was a gigantic dime museum with nothing to pay at the door.

Burridge and I put our little gripsacks, containing twenty years' gatherings, in the custody of the Kanaka Custom House, and took a carriage for the hotel. The drive was a pleasant one, some parts of the town looking like New Orleans, but the balance resembled Honolulu more than any place I have yet seen.

There was another shock lying in wait for us at the hotel. It was nothing like camp-meeting, and the landlord didn't blow on a conch shell to call us to dinner, and the guests didn't all sit around and eat with their fingers out of the same gourd. I had dreamed of lying under a jujubu paste tree with my mouth open to let the gum drops drop into it as they ripened and fell. I even thought we would have to dig our own bananas for lunch and climb a cocoanut tree for dessert.

The only real novelty offered us was a Chinese hotel clerk. There were three or four American clerks, but the belle of the lot was the Chinaman.

I have chased around foreign climes before now, with a lean gripsack and a yearning for home, hunting up a night's rest on the European plan, and met many brands of clerks. I have gazed into the glaring eyeballs of the fierce New Jersey clerk while my celluloid collar rattled inharmoniously around in the basement of my black, shiny, self-inflated grip. Incidentally I wish to state that it is ever safer to carry a valise which is obese in appearance and looks heavy by sheer

native force of character and pasteboard stiffening—one which bulges just as much when filled with smoking-car atmosphere as when surcharged with gold bullion and diamonds in the bulk. Those accordeon action grips are a mistake to a man who has to financier his way through life.

But I was talking of clerks and meant to say that I had had it out to a finish with the deadly English female clerk who draws beer with one hand, makes tatting with the other, and keeps books on a slate with her nose.

I have been made to feel how slight a thing is all human greatness by the Continental clerk who declines to tell you the amount of your bill unless you tip him or her for it. But I never yet struck a clerk who dazzled without paralyzing, as did A. Sing of the Hawaiian hotel. It was worth a 4,000-mile trip to hear him bang a bell and yell " Flunt !"

We asked Sing to get our things out of the clutches of a custom house which seemed unduly inquisitive about my tooth brush and my other collar.

We left him inserting foreign language into a telephone which seemed to be an accomplished linguist, for it worked just as well as when English was used. When we returned, he said :

"Flunt!"

" I have telphone moan six times flo yo slings. Th' cussem house plobably wear'n 'em." Sing had been graduated from the laundry business, and knew how it was.

Cap͡t. Cook's Monument
The spot where he was killed.

CHAPTER III.

Mainly Historical. The Discovery and a Naming of the Islands by
Captain Cook. His Fatal Mistake.

HE contumely which has for
ages been heaped upon the
ossified sandwich of railway travel has rendered
the term "sandwich" ex-
tremely unpopular on the
Hawaiian Islands. The natives seem to feel the disgrace keenly. Any young man who goes out there
and expects to be received into good society will find

it advisable to feign ignorance if anything in the sandwich line be forced on his attention. This circumstance
came near getting us into trouble. Burridge has long
been addicted to the ham sandwich vice. Almost any
hour of the day in Chicago, if he were seized and
searched, what is technically known as a "hammer" or
"corned beefer" might be shaken out of his clothing.
He was gently warned about it when he reached here,
but he persisted in flaunting his food in the face of a
muttering populace.

"This is a bluff," said Burridge. "I don't believe
they will do anything."

"That is what Cook thought when he was here,"
put in Barrister Peterson.

"Cook? What Cook? You mean the Cook's
tourist man?"

"No. Cap Cook, old Cap Cook, who came here
first. He discovered the islands and the natives didn't
kick very hard, but he made his mistake when he tried
to name them the Sandwich Islands. They didn't
like the name."

"What happened to him?" asked Burridge, getting
interested.

"Oh, nothing much—they don't call it much here.
The first time they caught him out alone they hit him
with a base-ball bat all covered with warts and bun-
ions and they filed the clothes off him with a pole
covered with shark's teeth all sticking out. He squirmed
around some, for the teeth ripped up furrows on his
hide like a patent corn planter, and so they impaled
him to the earth with spears like three-pronged har-
poons, or lightning rod tips."

"That was fiendish!" exclaimed the horror-stricken
Burridge.

"Well now, you couldn't blame 'em much, you see,

he used the term 'sandwich' on 'em without their consent."

"What became of him?"

"They got a flat stone and put it an his head and piled lava on it until his skull began to crunch."

"Did that kill him?"

"Oh, no; not yet. You see, the native Kanaka is naturally a polite and light-hearted being, although he is terrible when he smells a sandwich. Cap Cook had by this time got restless in the legs. They have a spear they catch squid with, and they stuck several of them through his legs into the earth. When they did this Cap remarked, "Well, boys, I'm not kicking."

"Oh, this is awful!'"

"As I said before, the Kanaka is polite and accommodating. The weather was close and they took a cord or so of stone off Cap's head to give him air. Then they offered to send home any messages, collect,

Death of Captain Cook.

that he might wish, and to see that his last words were correctly reported for the Honolulu Morning Advertiser. Then they asked him how he liked the climate. You see there is nothing of which the Hawaiian, whether he be native, domesticated, or recently imported, is so proud as his climate."

"What did he say?"

"He was English, you remember, and tourists of that nationality are not very social, as a rule. Cap Cook's insular reserve was not broken through, even with a native meat ax. Some men never are social, you know. His lack of geniality hurt the natives, and they piled the stone back on his head and a poi fed native sat on the crest of the pile and sang the latest popular song,—one of those songs, you know, that are so popular that the singing of them disrupts families and breeds homicide."

"When Cap heard the song he hollered 'enough!' He was pretty feeble by this time, and as a native happened along with a calabash of melted lava which he had just got from a neighboring flow, they put it to the Cap's lips with the invitation to 'drink hearty.' He did so and was heard to murmur, 'I wonder how that Peoria whiskey got here.'"

"Yes, go on."

"Then the lava hardened on his insides and he didn't converse any more. The natives probably thought it was his English hauteur coming on again, and it angered them. You have seen a man who is no carpenter open a can of corn beef with a blunt-edge case knife. Well that is the way the Kanakas went prospecting in Cap Cook's vitals. The ax they used was a stone one, and was a very dull and unworkmanlike tool. They haggled too much for comfort."

"Brutal!"

"Yes, the ax might have been a little sharper."

"I mean the whole thing is horrible."

"You forget," remonstrated Mr. Peterson, "what provoked the deed. You forget Captain Cook's attempt to force an offensive name on these fair islands. You forget the effect of the name or the appearance of the sandwich has on native character usually so docile."

During this recital of the fate of the discoverer of the Hawaiian Islands, Burridge grew as pale as onefinger poi. He excused himself, slipped away and taking his choice private stock of sandwiches, temporarily secreted it between the mattresses of my bed.

When darkness came on he sauntered out of the hotel with a package under his arm and the assumed nonchalance of a desperate man. He skulked down alleys, and avoiding the glare of the electric light, headed for the sea.

I was not present but I suppose there was a shadowy figure seen for a moment poised on a rock against the sky, a deep wail of anguish o'er the parting, the splash of a heavy object tossed into the bosom of the deep, and the restless waves closed over the secret of Burridge's crime.

At any rate he came back from his night trip ostentatiously eating a banana.

Road to the Pali.   A Native Equestrienne.   The Pali.

CHAPTER IV.

THE town of Honolulu has solved the problem of rapid transit. It has done so by never being in a hurry, which is the easiest way out I know. And yet every one rides. No one with any social prestige—no one with any social pull ever thinks of walking. If you don't own a carriage you ride in a hack. The hacks here are very nice, and I discovered that when the Niagra Falls hackman dies he goes to Honolulu.

The natives ride horses just like cowboys. This statement includes the female natives as well. It is a common sight to see the coy Kanaka maiden of 250 pounds sitting astride a 225-pound horse, and getting speed and action out of it which is truly surprising to a humane man. In fact the habit of riding astride has been adopted by a great number of white ladies.

It is easier on the horse, which doesn't count. It is immeasurably safer for the rider, which also doesn't count. It looks infinitely better than side-saddle riding, which counts for everything.

But to go back to the subject of rapid transit.

Our first discovery was to the effect that the debilitating seeds of Anglo-mania seem to have been planted in Honolulu, for they call their street cars "tram-cars," or "trams." Such shameless abandon could not be outdone in New York.

With the spirit of investigation strong within us, Burridge and I, as early as possible without exciting

"The Kanaka Belle's Rapid Transit."

suspicion, started out to do a little business with the Honolulu street cars.

We boarded a bobtail about 9 o'clock of the second evening of our arrival. The passengers dropped out early in the game, but we resolved to see the end of the line.

The course ran through tropical gardens, and after awhile the electric lights got scarce and things seemed lonesome and sad.

"Following The Iron 'Spoor.'"

We could hear the sea moaning like a man whose wife was chasing around the neighborhood to borrow a peppermint bottle for him. The tropical foliage along the sides of the road swayed and beckoned in the breeze like hackmen who are forbidden by ordinance to "accost the traveler or solicit patronage by word of mouth," as the law reads in some towns.

The tram-car meanwhile rolled placidly on.

The moon became obscured behind a cloud, and the wild note of the tulu bird quivered on the night air like the yelp of an amateur flutist who is hit by a brick and does not let go the instrument.

The car jogged around corners so many times that we couldn't tell which way north was. Experts in getting lost have assured me that there is nothing which gives a lost man so much pleasure as to know where north really lies. He may not be able to use it in his business, but still it is a great comfort.

The situation was becoming strained. We were both suspecting each other of unpardonable ignorance on the subject of our whereabouts, when Burridge asked:

"Know where we are, Jones?"

"This is a new one on me; do you know?"

"No-o. His voice trembled like a fat man's shirt-stud at a minstrel show. I saw he feared the worst. "But we can ask the driver."

"Yes, that's so. You can ask the driver."

"You better ask 'im."

"Aw, no, you do it." Our previous communication with the Kanaka driver was of painful character. All the English he used was composed of cuss words which he festooned on the corners of the mules.

Burridge will go to his grave in a doubtful frame of mind whether he was insulted or not. You understand we got in, put our nickels in the slot and rode awhile; then the Kanaka opened the door and said something we didn't understand.

Burridge asked me to translate it, and I told him that he was using Professor Garner's monkey language on us. He got mad at being taken for a gorilla, and every time the driver looked back, Burridge wrinkled up his nose and shook his fist at him, we being the only passengers. He, however, kept ringing a bell, and we tried some more nickels in the slot. This appeased him, and he transferred his thoughtful consideration from Burridge to the off mule.

Burridge agreed after some urging to try the Indian sign language on the Kanaka. He moved up on him and began to draw circles in the atmosphere with his forefinger, all the time showing the whites of his eyes like an amateur Lady Macbeth. Then he whirled around like a ballet-dancer.

All this was to signify that we were turned around, but the Kanaka did not stop to figure out the combination. He backed off the platform and melted out of sight like a $10 note in the glad Christmas tide.

Burridge looked at me and I looked at Burridge. The great, crushing truth came home to us simultaneously; we were 5,000 miles away from home and lost— lost in a tram-car.

Burridge recovered the use of his voice first, but it came brokenly. "I have heard," said he, "that mules have been eaten in cases of emergency, and that they sustain life for a long time."

"The Horse with Anglo-Mania."

The idea was not inviting. It was even less so when I went out and looked at the animals, which were settling on their foundations. Ossification had already set in.

"We must have courage," said Burridge, "and face

this problem. If we only had a turn-table we might escape that mule-chop breakfast. But we haven't got it. We seem to have acquired the street car all right, but the blamed thing is headed the wrong way. What will we do?"

I couldn't see much *bon vivant* business in the mules, and voted for adjournment in the general direction of Honolulu's trade center.

He agreed to this and wrenched the car lantern off its perch, and we started back in some doubt. Let it be confessed that we had not gone far when Burridge stumbled. He looked down and there was the street car track.

"Ah, ha!" he exclaimed, "here is the iron spoor of the tram-car, as my friend Haggard would say." After this discovery the rest was easy.

We tracked back and reached the hotel at about midnight and told Landlord Johnson about our getting lost. "Why in Sam Hill," said Johnson, "didn't you ask your questions in English? The company is an English one, and all the employes are required to use the English accent during business hours."

It was the Cockney patois that we failed to recognize at first. But the end was not yet. The next morning we were visited by the police. The charge, if I remember rightly, was stealing and otherwise feloniously abstracting a street car, vi et armis, with two certain draft mules, which were described in glowing colors and much forensic eloquence.

There was a second count which charged us with intimidating and threatening to do bodily harm to one Delancey Marmaduke Paha, to his great pain of mind and body.

It seems that the Kanaka had escaped to the city and reported that two Howris (foreigners) had boarded his car, and that one took a strong dislike to him from the start. This one was a prayer killer and proposed to do him to death by certain voodoo incantations.

It must be explained that no matter how civilized a native Hawaiian may become there is always in him some remnant of the old barbaric superstition. In the old times if a Kanaka was wronged by another the wrongee announced that he would pray the wronger to death in, say one week or ten days. He,—the prayer killer,—went out and built a little shelter in sight of the domicile of his victim and went to work, while some of his friends held the watch. Almost invariably the object of prayer sickened and died within the prescribed time. It was merely faith cure reversed.

This is now believed to be an obsolete custom, though back in the interior of the big island of Haiwaii it has been successfully accomplished within the last few years. The street car driver merely thought that Burridge was trying to voodoo him.

I discovered early in the day that I would have to learn to ride if I didn't want to miss a lot of good times with poi on the side.

It is the proper thing to visit the Pali, which is an institution located at the end of a seven-mile mountain road. The correct way to go is on the upper deck of a docile horse.

When a party of ladies and gentlemen was made up for a Pali picnic and we were invited, it was taken for granted that my other name was Broncho Bill. I hesitated over undeceiving them, for they seemed so happy in their delusion.

I did not feel like telling the ladies that the last time I was on a horse was ten years ago in North Dakota, and the brute hurled me over his head into an alkali slough. My brow was inserted in the mud about two feet, which left my anatomy waving in the breeze like a stunted two-pronged tree denuded of its leaves in the pathetic autumn time.

Since then I have often thought I would like to get an elephant howda and lash it to my horse before I tried it again.

But the ladies gave me a jar of olives and some other plunder to carry because I was such a good rider.

I may as well state that the uncultured natives along the line of march complained that the plums which they found by the roadside had been spoiled by the salt ocean water.

When the morning of the picnic arrived and I was led out to my horse, we looked each other over with mutual contempt. He was not a beauty. He was not the noble animal of the first readers. He had a divorce court temper and more angles than a problem in the back part of the geometry.

The ladies told me to be careful of the olives and galloped off. I affected to be busy tightening the animal's corset in order to put a little distance between us.

When I first attempted to get on board, the horse moved and spoiled the picture, and I found myself astride a section of thin Honolulu atmosphere which didn't seem substantial enough to bear my weight. I finally managed it without the aid of a step ladder and we started. Then the infamous beast commenced to trot.

I tried to induce him to keep step with me, but he wouldn't do it. When I was going down he jumped up and met me. We came together with all the force and warmth of old-time friends who had not seen each other in years. Thus he played lawn tennis with me—and he was an expert—keeping me dancing in the breeze for seven long miles.

I found that he too was affected by Anglo-mania. The way to steer was not by hauling on a line in the good Yankee fashion, but by pressing the ribbons on his neck as they do in Rotten Row. We, the beast and I, found ourselves in the track of an oncoming street car, and I tried the American system of steering, with a touch of Delsarte thrown in as an inducement.

I didn't know exactly how it happened, but I found myself jammed against the car, and it nearly tore me out of the saddle. The next day a bill came in for paint which we, the horse and I, had scraped off the side.

The guide books say that the scenery to be viewed on the road to the Pali is of unsurpassable magnificence and grandeur. I am not in a position to affirm or deny. I was too busy keeping my tongue from getting between my teeth, in which event there would be no saving it.

The ladies were very kind to me when they discovered how I rode, and nearly fell off their horses with inward and supressed mirth.

They worked hard to keep my feelings from being lacerated as much as the rest of my person; but when at a distance I heard a snicker like the tearing of 6-cent cambric I knew that my equestrianism was the fascinating theme of the snicker recital.

We reached the Pali in due course of time and lunched without olives. The mountain top was enshrouded in clouds, and one was able to see about three feet.

The view presented was a perfect counterpart of that seen in the steam-room of a Turkish bath with everything in full blast. Coming down the mountain I got a club in the hope I might score something against the pounding the horse had given me. He skated down in a mighty brief space of time, which was the only agreeable feature of the performance.

A Kanaka Home.

CHAPTER V.

American Ideas Prevail—State and Historical Secrets Never Before Divulged—The Army of the Queen—Studying for a Courtier.

EVERYTHING was American on the Islands even long before annexation was considered, from the genuine American French on the hotel bills of fare down to the Fourth of July, which was celebrated during royal rule with an oration containing the latest news from Bunker Hill, with a brass band, a greased pole, and all the other accessories for the proper development of patriotism, including the next morning's case of dislocation of the hair.

In fact, the town is so American that a man keeps forgetting that it was ever anything else. The last specimen of royalty was Queen Liliuokalani, the sister, not the wife—as many suppose—of the late King Kalakaua. There are enough princes and princesses for fairy tale purposes, but I did not hear of any dukes and lords. It must be remembered that the resources of the islands were largely undeveloped, and this must not be laid up against a new country struggling along on canned corned beef and living on the prospects of a boom in the spring. Let us be patient with the Hawaiian Islands and all will be right in time. There were a lot of marked-down, fire-sale nobles who were elected for life and who met when the legislature did, running a side show which corresponds to the English body of divorce court stars and swell hoss jockeys known as the House of Lords. No one heard very much about the Hawaiian House of Nobles, and when there I advised it to advertise liberally in the newspapers for business and have its diamonds stolen or something of that sort if it wished to get to the front. The violet-eyed modesty of the upper Kanaka house did, in its time, give it a mighty low rating in Bradstreets. I had always felt an insane desire to josh the nobility, but restrained myself when any one was around, for there is no telling but that my hack-driver might be a noble in disguise, and I would have hated to hurt his feelings. It is hard enough to be a hack-driver.

A few years ago the Hawaiian monarch was very much more of a personage than during the last inning.

18

There was a revolution in which old man Prerogative got the sawdust kicked out of him. It wasn't much of a revolution, as revolutions go, there only being a half-dozen men killed, but it worked like a charm.

The government had been trying to maintain its position in society with a constitution which was shiny in the seams and bagged in the knees in a way that was a burning shame. The King thought it ought to

The Birth of Constitutional Liberty. •

do until he sold his hogs and could afford another, but the populace, which was up to the times, insisted on the latest style right away, and didn't want any installment payment plan either. The King said he wouldn't have it, and both parties clinched on this proposition. Kalakaua returned to the palace, which is in a large garden, and was at that time surrounded by a fifteen-foot wall. He got the family cannon out on the piazza and trained it on an adjacent livery stable. I never could understand what he had against that institution, but possibly he had ridden in one of its hacks. The standing army, which was with him on the piazza, was instructed to plug the daylights out of that livery stable, and strike a blow in the name of Hawaii and its royal ruler. Then the King retired to commence his day's work.

While the proprietor of the stable was chasing around like the foreman of an amateur fire company, yelling, "It is all a mistake; my stable don't need any ventilating holes shot into it!" and begging the army for heaven's sake to turn the nozzle of the instrument the other way, a little band of patriots, with their shotguns, mounted the roof of the Royal Theater, a building across the street from the palace. The situation commanded the whole grounds, and when one of the army stepped out to fire the gun he was picked off by the party on the roof. This act was painful to some, but it was popular with the masses, and was encored until five soldiers were killed. Artillery practice then became so unpopular in army circles that it was regarded as a bore and temporarily given up. The

King retired to his private bungalow in the palace yard. The insurgents learned this, and they lighted Chinese bombs and threw them on the roof of that edifice. These bombs are noisier than a labor agitator, and their explosion on a tin roof was worse than a band tournament. No one can play poker with any degree of comfort under such circumstances, and Kalakaua was very much annoyed at it.

"Ho, varlet! Tell those folks in the flat above," the King absent-mindedly remarked, who was much engrossed in his game, "that they must keep their kids still or I will see the landlord."

"But it is the rebels, your Highness, and they are letting off fireworks at us."

"This is no flambeau club, and I want it stopped," returned the King in some heat.

"They won't stop until you sign the new constitution, your roy'l highlights."

"Well, fetch them in. I suppose I might as well sign it to get rid of them." Then the minions went out and borrowed a poi sign and waved it o'er the palace walls. A white flag, it must be explained, is always an indication that poi is for sale in this country.

The spectacle of royalty brought to bay is ever a pathetic and interesting one, whatever be the sympathies of the onlookers. Oliver Cromwell chasing Charles I. around a pasture lot with a pair of handcuffs, and Louis XIV. trying to dodge a party of vigilantes with a rope are to me the most exciting episodes of history, and the incident of Kalakaua being made to jump so high that his head knocked down the plastering of the

The Army Swooned.

ceiling, by a Chinese bomb explosion, is one which travels in the same class.

"Come in, gentlemen," continued Kalakaua, as the revolutionary party appeared with a new-laid constitution under its arm. "Let's get through with this business for I have just got the best hand I have held this week and I want to see if it is any good."

The rest was easy.

"Ah, um," continued the King, stroking his whiskers, "are we all in? Oh, sign the constitution? Certainly, certainly; in a minute—give me one card—Oh,

Burridge's Second Battle with the Army.

yes, yes, where do I sign—here? Yes—I'll have to raise you I guess—I hope that signature is satisfactory. Good day, gentlemen," said the shorn King, picking up the hand he had lain down. And thus was constitutional freedom secured to the Peaceful Isles, which are only menaced now by the military, and that usually on dark nights.

During the period of our investigations the Queen forced the army on our notice several times. The standing army, which, by the way, sat down most of the time when folks were not looking, had since the days of the revolution been recruited up to its normal strength, and counting all the non-commissioned officers, brigadier and major generals, numbered in full sixty-four. It was composed of Kanaka young men who were not fat. Their uniform was of white duck with cork helmets. They looked pretty well when not trying to toe a chalk line, which, though it was their great ambition in life, never quite achieved it. They didn't seem to enjoy the work, and in fact most of them soldiered their jobs. The Kanaka is all right on the score of individual courage, especially when there is a little excitement in it. In daring nautical deeds he is not excelled, but army discipline makes him shudder.

The major-general was as important as a young man who has for the first time been elected a parent by a bare eight-pound majority; but he had to walk with the rest of the troops. He had the advantage, however, of not being obliged to carry anything but his dignity and an obtuse, cross-cut sword.

We were watching a drill one afternoon and the troops did pretty well, considering that they were working by the day. They were not more than a minute tardy in working off their stint of evolutions. The general gave his orders in Kanaka language without being obliged to look on his book of tactics very often. During the drill, after giving his men orders to take aim, it occurred to him that he wanted to smoke. He drew a match down the stripe of his trousers, and while he was nursing it into action and looking cross-eyed at the end of the cigarette in his mouth, the guns in the hands of his troop commenced to give out signs of nervous prostration. The men in the rear ranks with the despairing calmness of veterans in battle who see the day going against them, hoisted the muzzles of their weapons on the shoulders of those in front, while the latter, without anything for rests, let the guns drop gently to the earth.

An evening or two after this Burridge and I were returning from a dinner in a carriage and again met our friends, the army, drilling under an arc street light. It did most of its work after dark, partially to avoid getting tanned by the sunshine and partially because the army looks better in the dark, and can chew tobacco while it drills without getting caught. As we passed it Burridge, in that frolicsome way of his which kept me continually sending our regrets to the police, stuck his head out of the hack and yelled at the soldiers. His shriek was like the fortissimo finale of a cat fight with all the stops pulled out. It was like a convulsion of nature when a new geological epoch is started. The citizens in that ward of Honolulu got out of their beds thinking a new brand of earthquake had struck town.

The effect on the army was electrical, as the patent medicine advertisements say. At the time Bur-

"Jones as a Courtier."

ridge caroled his roundelay the troops were in the middle of a comic opera evolution and consisted of a line of soldiers twenty long and two deep. The first line heard the noise first, naturally, and swooned in the arms of the second line. This was the only maneuver I ever saw them perform with anything like unity of purpose and uniformity of action.

A few evenings later another little incident happened which might have resulted in grave international complications. We were coming into town on a tram car and suddenly came upon the army again. It was occupying the street-car track practicing on the "West Point Glide" or something of the sort. The driver ground the crank and stopped. This infuriated Burridge, who, intoxicated by victory and emboldened by by his Napoleonic success as a tonic sol fa warrior, ostentatiously unscrewed the car. Whereat the general commanding planted himself in front of the mule and drew a long revolver which he pointed at the animal. This made Burridge thoughtful and he paused and looked at the Kanaka. He kept his yell in reserve, should firing be commenced, and with great presence of mind remarked: "Get out of the way, you Pullman car porter, or I'll run over you. Git up, mule!" Then the car started and the general stepped aside. In commenting on this incident the Honolulu Evening Bulletin suggested that for the safety of the populace it had better be made a misdemeanor punishable by fine and imprisonment, in the discretion of the court, for the standing army to carry firearms, or else it ought to be put under bonds to keep the peace. The Hawaiian army was a joke, and most people there grinned when they referred to it. But it was a necessary adjunct to royalty and lasted as long as royalty did.

The deposed Queen was very dignified and very punctillious in all matters of court etiquette. Like the tram cars and the horses of the community, she had Anglomania also, and worked her court on the English plan. During our visit she was in official mourning for her husband, the late John O. Dominis, an ex-American. It is not easy to be a queen, and she had to mourn according to the statute in such cases made and provided. Her time was nearly up, and she wept by law with one eye and watched the clock with the other. She didn't see company while her nose was red with grief, and that was why I was not presented to her. I rather expected to, and worked hard getting posted up on court etiquette. I practiced walking backward with a firm and confident air, which was somewhat marred by Burridge placing footstools and boots where I could hit them. He was anxious to have me perfect in my circus act, so that I could step on a royal poodle dog with *sang froid*, and not betray any plebeian Chicago breeding by sitting down on him. I was warned, if I stayed to tea, not to compliment the old lady on the rise of the biscuits or the cut of her preserves, for she probably would be as surprised at them as I might be. Now it is everlastingly too late. There is no hope of using the information and behavior on her that I so painfully acquired.

CHAPTER VI.

Down the Islands—Wrenched Apart from Honolulu—Victims of
the Lai Habit—A Dash of Geography—Landing Human
Freight.

HE volcano of Kilauea
—pronounced Kill-
away-ah—is the ob-
jective point of most
tourists who visit the
islands. There are two
ways of getting there
from Honolulu—one
by the Wilder Steamer
Company, which trav-
els down the windward side of the islands, and the
Inter-island Company, which operates on the opposite
side. It involves a trip of two days steaming and one
day horse-backing to reach the volcano, and however
one may make it, the trip is fraught with more variety
and incident than the job of taking nine small children
to the circus at one time.

The first hard work is for a fellow to wrench himself apart from Honolulu. If he made any friends
among the hospitable people of the town, and it is his
fault if he hasn't, they are all down to the wharf to see
him off and to give him advice on how to take a fall
out of that noted athlete, M. Mal de Mer—the reme-

dies recommended ranging from lime juice to suicide.

There is another very pretty and poetic custom
that the Honolulu people have adopted from the native Kanakas at the same time they adopted their land
and other trifles. This is the custom of decorating de-
parting friends with wreaths of flowers, spelled lais and
pronounced " lays."

One of the most picturesque sights of the city is a
sidewalk flower market, where native women sit on the
ground and string ginger and other flowers and mili
leaves to sell to those who have friends about to de-
part.

After the lines have been cast off and the voyage
has actually commenced the decorated tourist tears off
handfuls of the flowers and throws them on the wharf,
when they are scrabbled for by the original donors.
These sprigs of mili are then cherished religiously until
the absent one returns.

This custom, when tried on tender strangers like
ourselves, and the full force of the pathos of it striking
in, is more likely than not to create a feeling of sadness.

Burridge and I, of course, came in for decoration.
Our private flower mission did nobly, and we wouldn't
have been treated better had we been convicted mur-
derers in an American jail.

I was festooned with lais until all I needed was a
toy monkey on a stick thrust into my umbrageous
whiskers and a few wax candles to be a first-class
Christmas tree. Burridge looked like a popular prize-
fighter's funeral.

Then when the bell rang we leaned up against the
rail and sobbed convulsively in concert. It is the correct thing to do in this happy land of sentiment, flowers and poi. At home it might be considered unmaid-
enly to give way to grief before a large and critical
audience, but it is different there.

As the steamer Claudine moved slowly out from

22

the wharf what first appeared to be a number of floating cocoanuts bobbed up in the water below. They
were the heads of young Kanakas who were there to
dive for any silver coin which the passengers might
throw them.

As soon as Burridge understood this he stopped
snorting on my shoulder long enough to extract from

Shedding a Parting Tear.

me all the small change I had in my clothes, and in his
generous, free-hearted way chucked it overboard to the
boys, while my lamentations took on a new fervor and
a deeper meaning.

And so we started for the South, with the band
playing, handkerchiefs fluttering, hats waving, cries of
"Ahoha, good-by," shouted across the water, and a belated Chinaman fanned the atmosphere with an unre-
ceipted wash-bill, crying out for 75 cents or revenge,
while Burridge and I tried to assure him across thirty
fathoms of deep ocean that were good for even twice
that amount on our return.

There are five large islands and three or four
smaller ones lying in a procession from the northwest
to the southeast, about as irregularly as the Kanaka
soldiery on dress parade.

Counting from the north, the first one is Kaui, the
second, on which Honolulu is located, is Oahu—pronounced like the substitute of a cuss word when your
corn is trodden on in polite society—then comes Molokai, the island upon which the lepers are sequestered;
Maui fourth, and the big and comparatively new island
Hawaii last.

All are mountainous and rugged, being of volcanic

origin, but it is on the latter that the intrepid tourist
tracks the active, untamed volcano to its jungle lair.

From Honolulu to Hilo, the main port of Hawaii,
is about 250 miles. Frequent stops along the coast to
discharge Chinamen and natives and take on sugar
spins the trip out to a two-days' run, though it is frequently made in shorter time. The steamers are comfortable, being in matters of appointment, accommoda-
tions, food and service about like the average lake pro-
peller. There is something of a steam-barge rig
adopted, however, an open deck space being left forward to accommodate freight, which is the chief source
of revenue.

The sail down the windward side of Hawaii is
grandly picturesque. Beetling cliffs rise above the
steamer to a height of one and two thousand feet, covered with creeping vines and tropical verdure, while
peeping over the top are the cane-fields, looking for all
the world at that distance like Illinois corn.

Back of the cliffs rise the snowclad peaks of Mauna
Loi and Mauna Kea to a hight of nearly 15,000 feet.
Snow and rain fed mountain torrents tear down the
sides of Loa, and reaching the precipice plunge over,
one or two thousand feet, into the sea. In a morning's
sail we passed ninety-eight beautiful cataracts.

The steamer was riding the big Pacific swells which
rolled in on the rocks and broke in yeasty foam. The
scene was magnificent beyond the power of language

Lamb Tongue's Wash Bill.

to describe, and Burridge's artistic soul was so moved
that he got out of his bunk and borrowed my kodak
plug, which he rammed down his throat to keep his
breakfast corralled, and went on deck to enjoy the
beauties of nature.

There are no ports worthy of the name on the islands except at Honolulu and Hilo. It was therefore necessary to anchor the ship and do business with the shore by means of whale boats or freight boats built on whale boat models. It is in this kind of work that the native Kanaka is in his glory.

While the anchor cable is yet rattling in the hawsehole the native deck hands lower away the whale boats,

The Timid Freak.

no matter how high the sea may be running. This involves acrobatics of the monkey order, but it is as finished and graceful as the finest circus performance. But the Kanaka must talk and yell at his work, and it is carried on with a wealth of wasted conversation rarely heard outside a sewing circle under stress of excitement over the arrival of a new minister.

If there is something to be done and there is only one native to do it he will give himself the order in a loud and abusive tone of voice, acting in the capacity of second mate, and then as a plain A. B. seaman he will answer back and grudgingly obey, using back talk just within the lines of mutiny.

There are usually three or four boats at work, with six or eight men in each, all shouting like election night, and added to this are two or three outside boats from shore engaged in a polyglot yell recital in competition with the regular talent. It is a great place for deaf people.

Large numbers of steerage passengers are carried —Kanakas, Chinamen, Japanese and Portugese, the three latter nationalities being plantation laborers, brought there under long-time contracts.

The debarkation of these when there is a sea running forms a scene which is highly diverting when viewed, from the upper deck. The passenger climbs down the companion ladder and stands on the lower step. If the waves are big enough, one moment he is ten feet in the air and at the next he is water up to his knees. The whale boat is dancing in the vicinity like a man who has just sat down on the old homestead of a family of little busy hornets. When the boat nears the ladder about forty people yell "jump," and it is the passenger's business to shut his eyes and obey orders.

I went ashore at nearly every landing and learned that it was best to pick out a large, fat Kanaka and fearlessly leap into his soft, feather-bed anatomy. It was pleasanter for me, but it made big, ragged dents in the Kanaka.

One of the most exciting sights of the trip was the unloading of a female native who weighed 300 pounds if she weighed an ounce. She got down the steps with her baggage, which was promptly wrested from her and thrown into the whale boat. Then it

Umbrellas with the Soup.

swung up under the ladder for an instant, and every one shrieked "Let go!" but the old girl was timid and clung to the ropes. A second and a third time was the boat swung up to her, and she still feared to make the plunge. Then four of the boat's crew leaped on the ladder like big apes. One pounded her hands to loosen her grip, and the others seized her, and the deadly struggle began. It was like the hottest kind of a foot-ball rush. She was so fat that she was elastic, and was distorted by the pulling like an inflated rubber doll.

Everybody yelled.

At the brief instant when the boat was under the ladder the shapeless mass of Kanaka humanity fell off, struck the rail, and rolled to the bottom. The deck hand who acted as basement to the human haystack was dragged out and laid on some freight forward, so that he could get fresh air, while a kind friend shaped up his flattened ribs.

The Chinese laborers travel under the misfortune of not knowing either English or Kanaka. If they are new importations they have not learned the advisability of festooning their cues about their heads.

They are naturally a little backward over getting ashore, not having been brought up to an aquatic circus. If John hesitates, which he usually does, he is lost—doubly lost.

A sailor will leap from the rail to the ladder, grab the cue, and at the critical moment pass the end to a colleague in the boat. Then the hands "walk away with the slack" and John has to come, and he does come away from his fastenings with a rush. He may go overboard, but he is perfectly safe if his hair is planted in firmly.

These methods of debarkation do not apply to lady cabin passengers. They are placed in the boats and lowered by a steam winch, lighting on the water as easily as a sea gull.

We left Honolulu one noon and reached the terminal port of Hilo the forenoon of the third day.

It is a typical town of the tropics, lying on a bay, with a mountainous background. The islanders, when they have the energy, call it "beautiful Hilo," and the adjective is no misfit.

The business street parallels the horse-shoe of the bay, as in most of the island settlements. Untold millions of dollars worth of sugar has been shipped from Hilo, and yet there is not a sidewalk in the place.

The architects have builded with the fear of earthquakes before them, and the low building are almost universally embowered in tropical foliage of the richest kind. The soil is so prolific and the greenery so virile and of such spontaneous growth that when the Hiloan cultivates his garden he merely takes an ax and chops down that which he doesn't want.

There is a population of 2,000 or 3,000, a small but cultured American contingent being the dominant element. Hilo's glory is its rain, the annual fall being fifteen feet and some inches. We were in the place three days and caught about twenty minutes of sunshine in that time. The first thirty hours of our stay the rainfall measured $12\frac{1}{2}$ inches. When it is raining its hardest there a citizen doesn't dare go out with a cork life preserver on for fear he will be carried upward.

Our second dinner in the place was eaten under umbrellas, although there was an apparently good roof and we were on the ground floor of a two-story building. We procured slickers and paddled around in a gay, amphibious way with the hospitable inhabitants.

On one social occasion we were projected into the regular road-agent brand of church fair, with all the ensnaring pitfalls of the States. It was held at high noon and was a great success, a large amount of booty being realized to build an awning to protect the infant class not from the rain but from the sun.

The sun is seen so infrequently that I suppose the occasional sight of it terrified the infants.

We eventually got tired waiting for it to clear up, organized our caravan, and started on a thirty-mile ride up the mountains to Kilauea with light hearts and dripping whiskers.

THE BEACH AT HILO—

CHAPTER VII.

WE started for the volcano of Kilauea, Burridge on a sleek and knowing mule with a woven wire mattress back, and I on a white medieval gothic horse with a mighty slanting roof and a knobby ridge pole. We had planned to leave Hilo at daylight, but the spell of the country was upon us and 10 o'clock rolled around before we got on our way.

"We," in this instance, consisted of my artistic companion, myself, a guide so-called, and his first assistant tail-twister, who rode behind and massaged the two pack mules with a club.

Once out of the beautiful old town, with its picturesque buildings and luxuriant foliage, we struck sugar-cane fields, which extended a few miles only.

The road for fifteen miles was as fine a country driveway as can be found anywhere, and is being constructed by the government of scoria and volcanic sand, affording a bed nearly as good as asphaltum. It will be finished shortly, and one can then travel from Hilo to the volcano in a carriage. The way led across a river or two, a mountain torrent, by tumble-down, moss-grown native huts and through stretches of hothouse jungle full of gigantic reeds, and creeping vines, the tropical trees so strange to Northern eyes picked out with spots of violent, dazzling crimson. Then a sketch of open in which there were coffee plantations and bananas growing wild.

More forest less tropical in character, for the ascent, though so gradual as to be unmarked, had been a material one and the air was perceptibly cooler. The woods thinned as we went on and settlements became sparser.

At the last plantation we jumped a ditch and sitting on the horses robbed an orange orchard, but looked in vain for the old granger to appear with a musket and a bull-dog. Some one watched us from a distance and never even yelled.

Robbery on the islands hasn't anything like the

26

movement and wild joy in it that it has in the States. Personally I prefer the style of crime that is in vogue in Illinois, where we get our fruit a la dead rush with rock-salt on the side.

A gallop of a mile or two more brought us to a dense stretch of woods, sub-tropical in character, in which the carriage road terminated. Here when lunch was concluded, we struck out on the bridle trail, leaving the guides in the rear to battle along with the reluctant pack mules.

The ascent, when we left the woods, became more apparent, and the trail for the rest of the ride—some fifteen miles—was over a comparatively recent—speaking geologically—lava flow. It was so obcure in places that we needed a first-class Indian in our business a good deal of the time.

The Caravan En Route.

The wall of forest grew dim in the misty air, and we entered upon a world of ferns which stretched away, coarse and rank, into the narrow horizon on three sides. There were a hundred varieties, the most conspicuous being the tree fern, which grows a trunk for itself six and eight feet high, the leaves, which are large enough to be called branches, extending from the top like palm trees making a gigantic umbrella under which a man may drive on horseback. When the ferns thinned out the bare lava showed black and brown under the green.

As we progressed the rock gradually predominated. Imagine a slooping sea of soap-bubbles, each ten, twenty, thirty feet in diameter, solidified, and many cracked across the top, with ferns and foliage issuing from the crevices. Or better, imagine a lands-cape composed of burned molasses candy cooled so as to present a surface rough and ragged with its torturous serpentine shapes intact, all covered with stove polish and with a fringe of foliage issuing from cracks and cavities.

It was over this our trail lay, and our animals threaded their ways single file, up and down, to right and left, with all the dainty care of egg-dancers.

The rumble of subterranean waters frequently reached our ears. The horses' hoofs every few rods gave back hollow sounds indicating the titanic bubbles, on which we were, had a mighty thin crust.

Of course we got lost. Waiting for the guides to come up was out of the question, for they hardly expected when we left them to make the Volcano House that night.

Darkness was only an hour away, and it was commencing to rain. We began to realize that it was no joke to get mislaid in a country where there was no "Lost and Found" want column in which to advertise for ourselves, when we spied a Kanaka grass hut on a hilltop some distance away.

It was like a large shed with each end inolosed, the middle consisting of a sort of open hall.

I dashed up the hill while Burridge sat on his horse with an umbrella raised, warbling a few wild notes. His selection apropos of our situation was the one entitled "He Never Came Back." When I reached the hut and slid from the back of Cathedral there was no sign of life.

I started to enter for investigation and came on the body of a dead Kanaka man, clad in white from head to foot, and lying on a low dais in the hall. It was something of a shock. Presently several small children, big-eyed and shy, appeared one after the other. One of the eldest could talk a little English.

It was their father, she said who died that morning. Her mother had fixed the body for burial and had gone off to the neighbors to drum up a funeral. No, we couldn't do anything for them unless we should meet any natives and then we might tell them, if we pleased.

The dreariness and the loneliness of it was something appalling.

We pushed on to avoid a night in the rain on the mountain side. Our orders had been to "hammer the horses" every time we struck a piece of level trail a rod or more long. They were not hammered to any serious extent, although we obeyed orders implicitly.

The rain soon came down with the regular Hilo movement, and we had to fix up for it. Burridge clad himself in a pommel slicker—a yellow oil-skin coat of the mother hubbard order architecture, which covered most of the horse, as well as himself. At a little distance the combination looked like a rat lugging off a canvas-covered ham.

More preciptous climbing through tangled foliage. The way was frequently barred by spiders which had run webs across the trail like kite strings. The spiders themselves look like soft shell crabs, but they are not poisonous.

There is nothing in the fauna or flora of the island which is so, except the national beverage—gin.

Just as night was closing in we reached a good road which indicated that the Volcano House was but a mile distant. The annimals knew that there were oats at the end of it. We called in our umbrellas and tore over the home-stretch with a John Gilpin action and reached the hotel under the bright glare of the volcano.

Here we were comfortably housed and found it a first-class summer resort hotel and something of a surprise, considering its insolated, not to say exclusive, position in the world.

That is to say it looked like a summer resort hotel, but it was different in that one could get the comforts of life without being obliged to raise money by a chattel mortgage on the baby to satisfy a rapacious landlord. Beer, however, was 75 cents a drink. It was that which most forciably suggested the resort idea. I think a blue ribbon movement would succeed first rate there.

CHAPTER VIII.

The Secret of the Volcano.—The Hated School Marm and the Hand-Me-Down Educational Facts.—The Truth now first Told and the Secret Divulged.

HERE is one school marm whom I have remembered for the past quarter of a century with a sort of smouldering hatred. I think I was about 7 years of age when she shot athwart my small horizon. She wore her hair in a big bag of netting, for it was a few years after the war. I don't think I hated her for that, but more because of the missionary spirit which raged within her.

She seemed to want to assist me to narrowly escape the gallows. This involved keeping me in after school to either make me re-learn a geography lesson that I knew by heart except when called upon to recite or to administer certain reproofs which I seemed to need.

At a certain stage of the reproving process she used to weep on the top of my head and tell me how much it hurt her to punish me.

That I regarded as a worse lie than I could even manage myself.

I was pretty cheerful when the weeping commenced, for I knew that from five to seven minutes from date I would be let out, not, however, before I kissed her good night. Her mouth was like a slit cut in pie crust. Strange to say, this kissing annoyed me very much, and I wasn't easy until I ran out and expectorated and polished my lips with my coat sleeve.

She habitually wore on her otherswise pale cheek a drug store flush, and one night when I had repented of my crimes to the Queen's taste and she put down her corned beef lips for a kiss I stood on tiptoe and reached for that flush with a willowy, lissome moist tongue like a cow after a choice mouthful outside the pasture fence.

When I got out I was the envy of all the little boys because I could spit red.

This ended the kissing part of my education, which was short but bitter. I remember her most vividly, however, in connection with volcanoes, and her efforts to teach me something about them. The average round was fought out about like this:

" Now, Connie, you may answer. What is a volcano?"

" A volcano is—is—is—A volcano is—is—is—" Very long pause.

" A volcano is a mount—Can't you finish it ? "

" Yessum. A volcano is a mount."

" Go on—tain—mountain."

" Oh, yes, I forgot. A volcano is a moun-tain." Strong emphasis on the "tain."

" Which," continued the teacher persuasively.

" Which," I promptly responded.

" Now, Connie, what does it do ? Don't you know ?"

" It does—It does—does—I know, but I can't think just now what it does. It does sumpthin'."

" Yes, it does something. It belches forth—now, what four things does it belch forth ? "

29

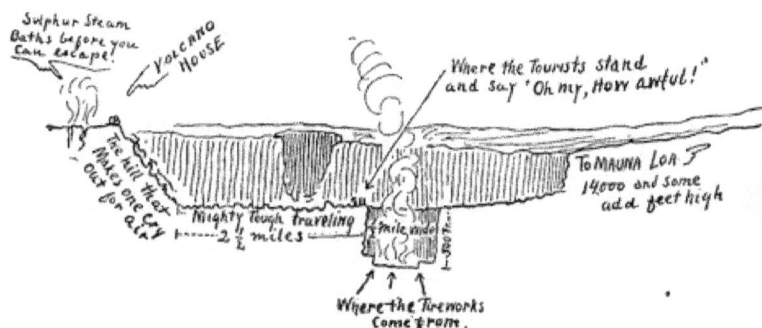

Sulphur Steam Baths before you can escape!

VOLCANO HOUSE

Where the Tourists stand and say "Oh my, How awful!"

The hill that makes one cry out for dear

To MAUNA LOA 14000 and some add feet high

Mighty tough traveling 2½ miles

⅓ mile wide

Where the Fireworks come from.

The Secret Exposed.

"It belches forth four things" said I, closely following the hot trail.

"But what four things?" Long pause again. Teacher sweetly asks again, "what four things?" Happy thought strikes me.

"Tar, pitch, turpentine an' lumber!"

"Oh, dear no,! They are chief products of North Carolina. Now what four things does the volcano

"What is a Volcano?"

belch forth. Just think" As if my poor hair wasn't getting loose at the roots with thought. She prompted me again.

"Fi-f-f-f—" and she made a noise like a mad cat, "Fi-f-f."

"Figs!" Trumplantly.

"Oh no, no. What warms you and cooks your vituals?"

"Ma does." This came doubtfully, for I didn't really believe my mother had been shot out of a mountain or she would have told me about it.

The answer seemed to discourage the good school marm and she said shortly: "It belches forth fire, lava, smoke and mud composed of ashes and hot water; now repeat it and begin at the beginning."

Then I answered in a loud and confident voice which diminished into nothingness before the sentence was finished:

"A volcano is a mountain what belts forth fire an' laughter an' smoke an'—an'—oh yes, an' mud, an'—an' that's all."

I thought of that school marm and her hand-me-down volcano information and how she used to send me to my seat when I forgot the mud, as I crawled out of a chilly morning.

I thought of her as I stood by the window, and gazed out over the many miles of lava waste and chased an erring gallus down my back. I thought of her as I tore around with an eye full of soap looking for a towel which my artistic partner has not used for a paint rag.

I wished she were there so that I could vindicate my recitation of the fall of 1867 and show her that I was perfectly justified in forgetting the mud.

In fact, Kilauea is enough to put the whole brood of geography architects to the blush. My confidence in them is mangled and bruised. My volcanic ideal, based upon Mr. Colton's once-popular work, is a tottering wreck. There is no mistake about Kilauea being the most prominent and enterprising of all the volcanoes on earth, and is the only one which never takes a vacation or shuts up for repairs and while Kilauea is on the side of a mountain—Mona Loa—it is of itself a big hole in the ground.

I think it will take a diagram to give an adequate idea of its size, shape, and commercial standing. It will be seen that the volcano house is located on the brow of an ex-cliff, 800 feet high; that is to say, the cliff has fallen in at this point in times past, and the rock has disintegrated enough to make a soil sufficient to support verdure and good-sized trees.

Down this slope runs a mountain path. It is a mile long, going down, and about five coming up. From the point where this path strikes the lava floor

Chasing the Erring Gallus.

to the pit which contains the molten lake is two miles and a half.

This lava floor, which from the hotel looks as smooth as an asphaltum walk, is in reality like Lake Michigan might be with the wildest cross-chop sea that was ever kicked up, solidified at the instant when it was at its height, and additionally cut and scarred by seams and big crevasses.

The tourist on his first visit requires a guide to conduct him to the liquid lake, for while the trail is much traveled, it is over rock, and therefore difficult for a novice to keep, but Mr. Lee, of the Volcano House, has recently set up a line of land-marks, which make it easy to follow on the second and subsequent trips, or after the way has once been pointed out.

We made several trips to the lake and I sat down and let my feet dangle over the edge and tried to think up a lot of hard names to call the angry red sea below me. I gave it up with a headache. I think that no one but a Hardshell Baptist preacher could do the subject justice off hand.

Speaking of that denomination, right there on the brink is the finest site for a chapel in the world. It is hard to believe but even Burridge expressed his intention of joining the church when he got home.

However, there seems to have been some visitors who were not awed into decent behavior. I refer to the abandoned advertising fiends who write their names on rocks.

To toil for hours over the lava and come on a big rock facing the volcano, on which is the pertinent advice, "Use Sudd's soap for eruptions," strikes one as bordering on contempt of court. Ben Hogan, somewhat known in America who did quite a lively business in Honolulu as a professional "exwickedest man in the world," as his bills stated, left his ad, which is a seven-column display, done in white paint on the cold brow of a rock.

Privately I think this was his culminating crime, and he needs to be reformed once more with a baseball bat. I had a chance to tell him what I thought about it and did so in no uncertain language.

Bound for the Brink.

I first however, took the precaution to put some distance and a small cliff between us, merely by way of giving myself time to apologize should he show symptoms of back-sliding into pugilism again.

These name-writing idiots keep Landlord Lee very busy chasing over the country with a pot of tar and a whitewash brush obliterating the little 10-cent bids for glory and immortality.

BURNING LAKE OF KILAUEA—

CHAPTER IX.

The Molten Lava Lake—Confidenced Again.

THEY had me scared in Honolulu. Whenever I got to talking about the then prospective trip to the volcano my friends commenced to eye those rare exotics, my feet. This made me feel coy and shrinking below the knees, and I toed in and modestly tried to hide them behind the furniture.

But this seemingly public interest in a strictly private affair was merely the preliminary to the question,

"How are you fixed for extra shoes? The lava, you know, wears one's shoes out like a file. You had better get an extra pair."

I heard this so frequently, from disinterested people who could have no interest in the shoe and leather trade of the islands, that I got in a sort of a panic, and toward the last they had me on the run.

I figured on being at the volcano some weeks and I calculated to make a trip every day or two, and each trip was to eat up one pair of shoes at the least.

I started in buying cheap canvas and baseball shoes in the Chinese quarter. Then I went up a notch and bought those mulatto shoes that tourists affect.

The shoe buying raged with great virulence and I got so that I could purchase footwear in the off-hand, careless manner of a cornless millionaire. They even got up a story that there was a revolution on foot and that I was a purchasing agent trying to divert suspicion by fitting out the army one pair at a time.

When we reached Hilo solicitous friends again urged on me the necessity of providing myself with more shoes.

They looked at my stock and laughed to scorn the dude product of Honolulu. What I wanted was brogans that would stand the terrific wear of the lava.

Visions of myself walking on jagged rocks like Washington's army at Valley Forge, with about an inch of flesh gnawed from the soles of my feet and with the bones sticking out in places, like the nuts in peanut candy, impelled me to load a pack mule to the limit with footgear entirely devoid of culture and refinement, but which they informed me was just the thing for leaping from crag to crag like the nimble gazelle.

After making my first trip to the burning lake I solemnly swore that I would jump in before I would follow any more friendly advice.

Her Shoes Were Protected.

I always had a kind of contempt for the stuff, but the trip confirmed my worst suspicions.

The next time I want advice I will go to some popular asylum and get it from the inmates of the incurable ward.

I started out loaded to the guards with shoes, but wearing an old Chicago pair. I tramped around shuddering at every leap lest the soles should come away from the uppers and expose my bunion to the critical gaze of a cold world.

I was surprised when I got back to perceive that my shoes were with me yet, and my surprise was mingled with pain when I remembered the gunnysack full of footwear on hand, for which I was doomed thenceforth to put up excess baggage charges. I made a number of trips, wore the same shoes and kept my bankrupt stock in the woodshed.

I wasn't the only one on whom the shoe dealers

danced with ghoulish glee. The other conspicuous martyr was a young lady from San Francisco.

She drew a pair of stockings over her shoes and then put on a pair of rubbers, a pair of her mother's stockings and a pair of her mother's goloshes, and then enswathed the whole in the gaudy remains of a bed quilt.

She walked down to the crater amid great excitement on account of the disguise, but became disgusted because the rest of our feet didn't bleed like a minority stockholder, and left the pile of hosiery and etceteras on the brink as a monument and a warning.

The regulation tourist making a quick trip usually arrives in the afternoon, takes a hasty lunch, and in company with guides makes the walk to the lake before dark, staying there until the shadows of night thicken enough to get all the effect of the fiery vision, which, with the darkness as a foil, is intensified tenfold.

After the visitor has looked until his eyes ache and his head reels, he is led back to the volcano house by the light of lanterns, where a sumptuous dinner awaits him.

Swearing Off on Friendly Advice.

This is the regular thing, though I was the humble instrument of adding a little to the picturesqueness of the trip. It was this way: Out on the cliff at the side of the hotel was a drying yard in which there was a clothes line that had strung along on it a number of those patent pinching clothes pins.

One morning a traveler from a place they call England, approached and asked me if I would have the keyndness to infowm him what those curious instruments were for.

The Human Guide-Book at Work.

"Why, certainly," I responded in my best Cook's tourist guide style. "Those little instruments are anti-inhalers."

"And, pray, what may that be?"

"You will find when you go down to the lake to-day," said I, "that the smell of sulphur fumes is very offensive and sometimes overpowering. These little instruments are designed to wear on the nose during the trip and prevent the odor making you sick. I would advise you to be sure and wear one or you may regret it."

"Really? It's very 'strawdn'ry."

"Yes, these are placed out here to air and so that the tourists can pluck them off the line on their way to the lake. It's very thoughtful of the management, I think."

He picked out a good stiff one and gave it to his valet to wash.

Two or three hours later I saw him at the crater with his pin on his nose giving out enthusiastic testimonials as to the efficacy and general reach of the volcano in a loud nasal tone of voice.

No two people when they return ever agreed upon the account of what they saw.

It seems to be a peculiarity of the volcano that it affects every one differently. The "descriptive writer" is an animal who wanderes down there with confidence born of inexperience and the chances are that his grip sack full of stock adjectives shrivel and wilt in the glare of Hawaii's pet wonder.

In the Volcano House is a visitors' book.

It is a cross between a hotel register and an autograph album. Tourists are wont to inscribe therein their feelings and impressions.

Many of them in a spasm of ecstasy over the hotel's noted "nice ohelo berry pie" eulogize it and forget the volcano; and most of them merely advertise their mental incapacity in this awful book.

The "descriptive writer" has rioted in its pages, but the only one who has in the remotest way approached the heights and depths of the subject left the following in the volume:

"Visited the volcano. It looks like hell.—John T. White."

In the face of such descriptive powers I feel timid about trying to convey an idea of the fearful pit.

After the theoretical shoe-destroying walk the tourist reaches the edge of the lake and stands behind a rampart of lava rock.

The cliffs go down sheer about 400 feet. Near the bottom is a ledge, which narrows the liquid part of the lake somewhat without detracting from the grandeur of the sight, for this big well is a half mile in diameter, though it looks much smaller.

"Enthusiastic Nasal Testimonials."

The liquid lava, on exposure to the air, quickly hardens into a thin dark purple crust, bordering upon black. Then cracks come in it like forked lightning against an inky sky.

These cracks widen and extend themselves until the surface of the lake is a network of red and white seams, separating the dark islands of lava, which have the identical form of ice cakes in a spring break-up.

Usually at or near the center muffled explosions occur every few seconds. A ghastly white fountain flings itself in the air, turns red and falls back on the commotion at the surface.

It is toward these explosive points that the lava cakes tend; they can not be said to flow for the movement is sluggish and as relentless as it is sluggish.

The pieces of lava cakes crowd each other in a horribly deliberate way and their edges are made jagged and curl up in the crowding.

They eat each other, some are torn and cracked and disappear under the liquid red, but always with a decorous slowness that somehow suggests untold reserved power. Occasionally an explosion of gas occurs under a cake and it is lifted like wet brown paper thrown by a tired arm. It may strike the perpendicular side of the ledge and there it sticks as though it were a rag saturated with glue.

Bluish flames flicker for a moment over the cracks, lighting up the cliffs. Even the fire fountains are in no hurry. After the thunderous boom which gives them birth the molten lava like the product of a smelting furnace at its highest heat swings upward, changing color as it goes, with the same appearance of oppressive weight.

The flickering light playing on the jagged cliffs suggests infinite possibilities in the realm of mystery.

The heat arising precipitates whatever moisture there may be in the air into a cloud, and so, hanging perpetually over the fiery vat, is a red and angry sheet of mist, which reflects back the uncanny light.

I tried to conjure up an adequate simile, and could think of nothing but a fight of overfed titanic reptiles of a past age, swimming in a sea of red paint, with lightning playing continuously over the scene.

A Cocanut Palm Grove.

CHAPTER X.

Good-bye to Pele.—Railroading down the Mountain.—A Human
Sandwich.—Self-denial of the Missionaries.

WHEN the morning came for our departure from Kilauea old Mauna Loa's slope showed still pink in the slanting sunlight. Below the cliffs the blackened pit smouldered sullenly and the lava fields looked like the flame-eaten ruins of a thousand homes. Madame Pele, the presiding godess of the volcano, has more moods than a spoiled child, and staying for months, we might have had a fresh menu every day; so it was with genuine regret that we began to pack, Burridge his acre or so of sketches, I my bag of shoes and half-barrel of lava specimens.

These, by the way, narrowly escaped being left behind for there was a cat, a moonlighter, with a rich contralto voice who under the lea of our bungalow poured out a passionate aria every evening, or so much of it as was possible before Burridge filed a hard, rocky, pound and half objection on the car's anatomy. My lava half bricks were altogether too good to last. But this is getting away from the subject.

Our return to Honolulu was over a different route from the one taken in going, involving a thirty-mile ride by stage and railroad down the leeward or dry side of the island to the port of Punaluu: thence northward along the coast for a day and a half of steamer travel. This way of returning completed an entire circuit of all the islands south of Ohau.

The returning party numbered altogether four ladies and seven gentlemen. And it took a couple of carriages to accommodate it, with a saddle horse or two for the overflow.

The air was still and crisp and invigorating when we clambered aboard and waved adieu to the chief engineer of the volcano, Mr. Lee, and his family.

The ride was one of those pleasant things to remember but of no particular interest when described. The wagon trail led for most of the way over a flow of lava and was in it way full of more ups and downs than a political career in a doubtful State. The road wound in and out canons, affording entrancing glimses of rugged scenery with here and there a sight of the blue Pacific glistening in the sun.

The way for the most part was lined with subtropical foliage somewhat sparse on account of the perpetual dryness.

36

There was a sort of enforce variety to the scenery, too. Just as a man settled himself to gaze on some delightful vista of hill and dale there would be a warning yell from the Hank Monk of a driver, and he would find his head pounding a merry tatoo on the roof of the stage.

When he struck the bottom again all the scenery he could see would be a gaudy astronomical display.

He Never Swore.

The government road now being constructed on the other side of the island will change all this in time.

About 11 o'clock the caravan stopped at a halfway house, which, in spite of a rather unpromising exterior, afforded a very fine roast chicken dinner.

It was kept by a hermit, so-called, a graduate of Oxford, who cooked the meals and served them himself. He satisfied himself with the society of a one-legged hen, and was apparently happy in it. The hen occupied the foot of his bed nearly all the time in a nest of pillows.

The mouth of a volanie cave, the remains of a subterranean lava river, is here, and its end has never been reached by man. Some of our party took a trip of an hour and a half's duration, reaching a spot where the roof was hung with delicate lava stalactites not larger than lead pencils in thickness, but several feet long.

A continuation of the drive for an hour or two over fine mountainside pasture lands brought us to a sugar plantation well down toward the coast.

Here we took the plantation railroad for Punaluu. Nearly every large one maintains its own narrow-guage road. These roads are frequently marvels of erratic engineering. The right of way dodges and shies like a cow being chased out of a garden. The speed, of course, is not great. If it was it would be like the game of "crack the whip."

The man who originally surveyed the road must have been following the trail of a wild goat which was laboring under great excitement.

It was at this plantation that I was made the victim of other folks' gallantry, or a low-down trick, I don't know which. The train consisted of a dozen coaches, the rear one only being covered and having seats. The rest of them were about the size of hand cars without the pumping works.

We gave up the first class coach to the ladies and three of us tried to make ourselves comfortable on a flat car. Just as the train was about to start two belated Kanaka ladies came puffing up.

There was no room left, and Jim Williams, the Honolulu photographer who was sitting beside me, arose with his usual courtesy and gave up his seat. Burridge, not to be outdone in gallantry, did likewise with the other.

The supply of Kanaka females gave out at this juncture, and there was no one left to whom I could

A Kanaka Postoffice.

relinquish my seat. So I sat there like a small piece of lean meat in a mighty thick human sandwich.

The two ladies were even beyond the regulation weight of 250 pounds and the thermometer registered something in the nineties, for we were pretty far down toward the sea level.

Every time the train went over a gorge my seatmates nestled up closer and seemed to regard me as the only sure preventative of a serious railroad disaster.

When we neared a precipice one of them persisted in grabbing me in a blood-boiling clutch.

I asked her kindly not to do it. I explained to her that I was no parachute and was of no earthly utility in a mad leap through space, but my protests were of little or no avail.

I did not enjoy the ride though Messrs. Williams and Burridge seemed tickled to death about something throughout the whole nine-mile run. And our ladies in the rear coach too seemed to see a good deal in the barren landscape that was uproriously funny.

I wanted ice and I wanted air pretty badly all the way, but there was one consoling thought: Mrs. Jones was not present to accuse me of flirting.

Tropical Transit.

Punaluu, reached in the middle of the afternoon, is a native settlement of some size and has a hotel which is surprisingly well kept.

In fact this feature of Hawaiian travel is something that excites constant wonder. A plunge bath, a walk on the beach, a good dinner and some Kanaka music in the evening occupied the time very pleasantly until the hour of retiring.

That night the steamer Hall came down the coast and anchored in the roadstead. At 3 a. m. her whistle was blown as a signal for the embarkation of passengers.

It was necessary to get on board before dawn, as the morning breeze kicks up a sea that makes the operation not only unpleasant but dangerous. Our party piled out like people at a fire, and after a cup of coffee and a light lunch, made for the pier.

The Kanaka crew had been handling freight all night, and we went off to the steamer in the last freight boat. Then the trip northward commenced, just as the sky was getting pink in the east.

Landward, thirty miles up the mountain, the angry glow of Kilauea was visible against the clouds. Most of the passengers turned in to finish their night's rest, but the rocky wall, fringed with green on one side and the glories of a tropical sunrise on the other, afforded plenty of inducement to stay on deck.

Our course lay all day along the rugged coast of Hawaii, with stops at frequent intervals. Early in the afternoon the Hall rounded a rocky headland and put into Cook's Bay.

It was here that the great circumnavigator and discoverer of the islands met his death. His compatriots have marked the spot with a monument of light stone, and the place is one which tourists make an effort to visit.

A rude rock and log pier, two or three houses, a chicken yard and the monument are the "chief objects of interest," as the guide books are wont to say.

There is a postoffice here, as there is at nearly all the landings. Burridge had developed a mania for mailing letters to his friends and enemies from all sorts of inaccessible places. His correspondents had about run out when we reached Cook's monument; but he managed to scratch off an impassioned appeal to his Chicago washwoman, praying her to return that missing half-hose so that he could have it when he got home.

This had to go with the monument postmark on it. We went ashore in the whaleboat and hunted up the postmaster, a mild-mannered old gentleman who aimed to please and merit a continuance of our patronage.

We found the P. M. on the pier, with the rest of the population, his handfull of letters made up and ready to be taken by our steamer.

Burridge insisted that his washlady would fret unless she heard from him direct from Cook's Monument and prevailed upon the aged man to go back to his house, get the postage stamp and take a hasty shot at it with the inkpad.

All this took time and when they returned the mate in the whaleboat yelled "All aboard," in a pointed and meaning manner. They scrambled over the rocks, the old P. M. endeavoring to make change as he leaped.

He missed his footing and went "bows on," as the mate expressed it, into a crevice between two large rocks while a wave came in and nearly drowned him. He was mute, but he turned to us a countenance working with the most frightful contortions as we lifted him out.

"What's the matter—lockjaw?" asked Burridge.

The victim shook his head.

We picked up the coin and letters, but still no word of execration. The old gentleman hobbled over the jagged lava and delivered his mail, working his lips but without emitting a sound.

"I wonder why he didn't cuss?" mused Burridge as we were pulled out to the steamer. Then on arrival he put the question to the captain.

"Was it the old postmaster?" he asked.

"Yes."

"He is a missionary. If he had cussed he would have lost his job. I tell you, the missionaries have a very bad time of it. I wouldn't be a missionary on just that account."

Later in the afternoon we struck even a more primitive postoffice.

It consisted of a rubber stamp, a box of shoe blacking, and a palm tree.

This postmaster sat on the ground with a piece of plank between his feet on which were the letters, and merrily plugged the portraits on the stamps with a grunt at every disfigurement.

He didn't look worried over politics and a change of administration had no terrors for him.

LOADING CATTLE.

CHAPTER XI.

The Hawaiian Steer—Gingery and Frolicsome—An Aquatic Bull Fight—Loading the Tree Roosting Cattle.

THOSE western parts of the islands called the leeward, or dry sides, along which our return voyage was made, supply magnificent but unworked stone quarry sites with incidental cattle ranches. These ranches, which have a slant like a tobogan slide, are composed of thousands of acres of brick-red soil from which spring rich, juicy jagged lava rocks, affording the cattle the greatest facilities on earth for scratching their backs

and sides. The Hawaian cattle, it is needless to say, are automatic curry combers.

Eating seems to be a secondary consideration. There is grass and herbage to be found higher up on the mountains but it is not visible except in spots from the coast.

Water is the serious ranch problem. I have seen cattle come down to the sea at low tide and stand knee deep in the surf and drink.

Before any one rises up and remarks that Jones is backsliding again in the trifling matter of veracity I wish to interpose an explanation and state that whether by instinct or simply by pure hustle, the cattle had found that there were springs of fresh water bubbling up under the salt and that is what they were after.

I waded out with a tin cup to 'try this drink, but not knowing as much about water as a year-old heifer with no school advantages I missed the spring and inadvertently quaffed a cupful of Hunyadi water, of which the Pacific ocean is composed.

They say that if shipwrecked sailors drink sea water they go crazy. I believe this and I know that nothing but the fact that I had not recently been shipwrecked saved my already tottering intellect.

The cattle we saw were wild-eyed and lean, and

40

had been trained down to make a mile in less than 2:10.

They look like overgrown greyhounds with horns. They shy and kick like a soubrette actress, and their kicks have all the sparkle and verve of those of a Missouri mule laboring under acute mental anguish.

At a comparatively recent date the algeroba tree was transplanted here, and on the dry side of the islands it thrives wonderfully. It will grow on soil which has heretofore only supported cacti.

The Cows Convulsed with Mirth.

Cattle and horses feed on the pods of this tree and fatten on the diet.

It is stated that these pods are identically the same kind on which the Prodigal Son lunched—before he went back to the old man for veal pot-pie and a new deal.

I tried to eat one. They have a mild, bitter-sweet taste, and are like petrified string beans cooked in cough syrup.

Since trying them I have even less respect for the Prodigal Son than ever before. If I had made a failure in the prodigal line of effort, it seems to me that about one meal of these "husks" would have driven me to the expediency of a sight draft on the old gentleman at once.

The algeroba tree matures enough to do business and shed its patent medicine fruit in about five years. It has a fine, feathery foliage and considerable barbed wire fencing concealed about its person which seems to resent familiarity.

One of the largest if not the largest ranch owners in the kingdom, is Sam Parker, a half caste, and the

last Minister of Interior under the Queen. He has sixty or eighty thousand head; he hasn't taken a census lately and no one knows exactly how many.

He told me that he had at one time an idea that he would like to market some of his cattle in Chicago, so he looked up Mr. Armour and commenced to talk business. He had a pretty large ranch, he said, and he would like to make a shipment. This was agreeable, and Sam asked how many head he should ship.

"I will take 40,000 a week," remarked the Chicago packer. "I wouldn't care to handle any more than that."

This ossified the big Hawaiian. When he recovered he told him that Chicago was too big for him. "Why," he added in telling the circumstance, "that man Armour would depopulate my ranch in ten days."

The leanness and activity of Parker's cattle has come to be a matter of public proverb and possible tradition.

He heard a short time ago that an acquaintance had bought some land and was about to start a ranch. The two men met in the streets of Honolulu. The Honorable Sam opened up with a proposition.

"Say, Colonel," he proposed, "I've got more cattle than I need. Let me stock up your ranch for you."

"W-w-w-with your k-k-k-critters?" asked the Colonel.

P. D. Armour Paralyzes the Hon. Sam Parker.

"Yes. I've got just what you want."

"G-g-guess not. It w-w-would k-k-cost too much."

"Oh, I can let you have 'em mighty cheap. I'm overstocked."

"N-no, g-g-guess not. Y-you see, I-I-I-haven't got any t-t-t-timber on my r-r-r-ranch an' it w-would k-k-k-cost too much t-t-t-to build r-roosts for 'em."

The island cattle are marketed in Honolulu, bringing from $30 to $45 per head, according to weight and condition. The chief item of expense is the transportation thither, which amounts to from $5 to $8 steamboat fare each.

One of the most exciting and characteristic sights of island life is afforded by the loading of the wild and kittenish steers on the steamers.

It takes on all the aspect of sport, and nerve-tingling sport at that. There is all the excitement of the usual round-up, with a strong spice of Spanish bull fight, a dash of aquatic athletics, with an occa-

A Night Scene in Parker's Ranch.

sional divertisement in the way of a free-for-all race, when a critter punches its way through the living corral and breaks for the hills.

When a bunch of steers is brought to a landing for shipment it is penned in a stone corral open on the sea, if there is one, and if not, which is usually the case, it is surrounded by a line of natives on foot and horse-back.

The Kanaka is a natural horseman, as he is a sailor, and rides with more of the abandon and grace of an Apache or a Comanche than of the usual white cowboy of the plains.

Just outside the curling breakers rides the steamer's whale boats ready to take the animals in tow. Then the word is passed and the circus commences.

With a whoop, which is used on all festive occasions in season and out of season, a stalwart Kanaka, pinching his little horse between his knees like a vise, rides into the herd and cuts out a steer.

He swings a lariat with a swish, and before the rope has settled over the animal's horns the little

broncho plunges into the breakers with the joy of a truant boy in swimming.

The steer bucks and prances and plunges, but with every leap the rope sags and the pony walks away with the slack.

The wildest struggles are adroitly snubbed on the pommel, and from the start it is a losing fight for the steer.

The bottom is rocky, rough and jagged. The pony is in deeper water and working against the waves, therefore at a great disadvantage.

A second cowboy spurs his horse into the fray. He leans over and grabs the steer's tail, which is pounding the air and water like a whip lash.

He loops the end of the tail and puts the bight around his pommel. This lifts the steer's hind feet off the rocks and he is slewed around broadside to the sea.

In jumps a nude native who splashes salt water into the face of the animal with all the vigor and effect of a burst in a fire pipe hose. At this point the fight is exciting in the extreme.

We watched twenty-five of these combats from a safe station from the rocks above, in the course of an hour or so.

From our post of observation the rocks formed an amphitheater with a seething foaming, bottom. In it the men, horses and steer were frequently an indistinguishable struggling mass of life. Big seas sometimes engulfed all the combatants, carrying them shoreward.

The period of time which a Kanaka will stay under water is amazing, not to say alarming. I saw a feat of submarine horsemanship which is not easy to believe.

A wave caught one of the riders broadside, and with the pulling of the steer on the pommel he was carried with his horse under water.

The next instant the horse's hoofs were visible, kicking above the surf. The next the rider rose to the surface on the opposite side from the one on which he went down, still in the saddle.

He had been rolled completely over, and blowing the salt water from his mouth and nose he let go of the lariat, which ran under his animal, caught it on the shoreward side, took a turn like lightning around the pommel, and plunged into the next sea apparently unconscious of the splendid feat he had just performed.

The water dashed in the eyes of the poor steer confuses him so that he can't tell the Pacific Ocean from Manna Kea.

He then becomes a comparatively easy victim. The cowboy with the tow line swims out to the waiting boat, and when the crew gets hold of it Mr. Steer comes away as though there were a turn around a steam winch.

He devotes his energies to just plain swimming, without fancy strokes. Arriving at the boat he usually attempts to crawl on board, but this tendency is discouraged.

He is floated around and stood on end in the

water with his back against the whale boat's sides.

If he has horns they are hooked over the rail and his head is lashed to the seat. His fore feet stick out above the water in a bless-you-my-children posture. When all the available space on the rail is festooned with steers heads the animals are towed off to the steamer.

They are then unlashed, floated under a block and tackle arrangement, where a sort of saddle is placed

The Captain Controls a Steer.

under them. This is hooked on to the tackle, the boatswain pipe is heard, and the animals are jerked upward, fighting like demons, and then lowered away to a point about a foot above the deck.

The lashing on the horns is then made fast to a spar running lengthwise and fixed at the proper height, their heads being hauled down as close to the spar as possible. They are then ready for the voyage. The whole operation is scientific in its way, and the speed with which a cargo of wild cattle is made up, consider-

ing the superior strength and fighting qualities of the animals, is simply marvelous.

It struck me as very brutal, but nobody has been able to suggest an improvement.

When one of the steers breaks out of the corral he is usually, but not always, allowed to go, for after a hot run, followed by a fight in the sea, the shock and chill of the latter frequently kills him. Out of the twenty-five cattle which were fellow passengers with us two died.

When the animals die they are gotten overboard as quickly as possible, for a death affects the survivors as though they were human. A panic seizes the bunch and they commence struggling at their lashings in a way calculated to move the beholder with pity and horror.

But once in a while the cowboys and sailors do not have it all their own way. We made the trip to Hilo with Captain Davis, of the Caudine

He had a big steer part its lashings after it had been put on board. The way it cleared the open lower deck was most beautiful to see.

The Kanaka sailors have a bright happy way of walking on the backs of the rows of standing cattle when at work. They do this to avoid the kicks they would receive if they went anywhere in the neighborhood of the loose end of the animals.

But this Napoleon of steerdom would not even allow that time honored familiarity. He tore up and down the deck with an undisputed right of way.

When a Kanaka sailor attempted to slip a noose over his wooly head he ducked and charged with a gallantry which brought cheers from the upper deck. The deck hands found it advisable to jump over and cling to the outside of the rail while the steer bumped his head against the bulwarks.

They ducked their heads when the shock came and bobbed up when it was over. The Captain watched this from the bridge with an impatient frown.

"I'll show you how to handle that steer," he remarked as he dropped down and advanced toward the bovine officer of that deck.

The steer stopped and returned the Captain's insolent stare in kind. Then, without any preliminary agreement, the pair commenced an exciting game of tag. The steer, was "it."

I think it was a matter of about ten seconds when the Captain was shinning up a spar and beseeching some one to call off the brute.

He was eventually lassoed and secured, but I stand ready to back Captain Davis to any reasonable amount in a Fourth of July greased pole climbing contest.

HONOLULU HARBOR FROM
PUNCH BOWL HILL.

CHAPTER XII.

The Difference between Stealing Wholesale and Stealing Retail Illustrated—The Hawaiian Navy and American ditto—Burridge and his Dress Suit—Naval Balls.

PON entering the port of Honolulu a second time we caught sight of the steamer which once constituted the Hawaiian navy. This ex-navy was painted a dirty lead color, was stripped of its warlike trappings and had been relegated to private life. It is now working the white-winged peace angle, as your sporting friend would say, and is fetching up from the islands cargoes of sugar, rice, paddy, bananas, coffee, cattle, poi and Kanakas.

The job is not nearly so gay as that of the old times, but it is less fretting to the owners.

The one-time navy looks like a Lake Michigan lumber barge after a bad season. No one would ever accuse it of having, in its mild youth, been long, low and rakish, and ready to belch iron hail should a foreign power intimate that the natives of Hawaii originally came from Africa.

This by the way is the deadliest output of the Kanaka insult foundry.

The old Kanaka kings had their navies, but they were composed of fleets of war canoes with out-riggers or rigged catamaran style and sometimes lateen sails.

The ambition fell to the late Kalakaua to have a real sure enough navy, with guns, and cannons and repairs and appropriations and all that, in the good American style.

Foreign war ships came into his harbor to maintain the dignity of their respective countries, and incidentally have a good time. They gave balls as well as ultimatums, and the Kanaka royalty, nobility, and gentry went off to the ships and danced and drank the punch, which is always full of action and enterprise in naval circles.

The late king thought it good, and desired to travel in the same class. Besides that he had a scheme to make the navy pay dividends.

The scheme itself was all right, but he forgot something. In fact, his early education had been not exactly neglected, but diverted from its proper chan-

44

nels. Had he but manicured his dark brown intellect in youth with a certain reading-book which gave me pain twice per day in the fall and winter of 1866, he would have known better.

In this book is a story which starts like a play, but has a sermon in its inside pocket. The scene is located somewhere in the suburbs of Greece. Alexander the Great, surrounded by men whose costume consists of a lawn-tennis shirt and a spear, all occupying the o. p. side. A clanking of chains is heard without. Enter r. u. e. what is left of a Clark street raid in the clutch of a big policeman anxious to do all the talking to the court.

Says Alexander with the rising inflection: "What, art thou that Thracian robber of whose exploits I have heard so much?"

He talked very good and grammatical English, considering he was nothing but a Levant dago.

Art Thou that Thracian Robber?

The robber speaks up: "I am a Thracian and a soldier."

The court sneers at this and the policeman starts in to tell how it was, but is shut off.

The robber doesn't try to beg off because he was full and had a hungry family, but starts right in with a campaign speech, comparing his record with that of Alexander.

He explains that while he has merely worked the sandbag in a humble but proficient way the great weeper has held up trains and tied express messengers to the floor. While he has gone with the gang and looted villages too small to have postoffices the great Alexander, who I also think was the original smart Alexander, feloniously appropriated to his own use, as the warrant reads, certain nations and countries.

He then made remarks about the difference between footpaddery for glory and for a living, concluding with some pertinent remarks as to the general nature and social standing of the hog.

This didn't strike Alec as good sense and they argued the matter over.

I don't remember what became of the gentleman from Thrace but I think the big General either held him over for trial or let him off on a suspended sentence after showing him his error.

The lesson somehow stuck in my young mind that the exact degree of criminality of crime in the public view depends not so much on the motive as on the size of the operation. I couldn't myself understand the difference, morally, between a Napoleon of finance and a common vulgar circus flim-flammer; but it seems there is a difference and courts and juries frequently discover it.

Now that is what ailed King Calico. He thought the Thracian was as good as Alexander, and the flim-flammer merited as much admiration as the N. of F.

He had seen England and France and Germany send out war ships, pick a quarrel with some South Pacific island king and proceed to seize his domain and rule it by right of conquest, which is the other name for wholesale sandbagging.

Down across the equator a couple of thousand of miles from the Hawaiian Islands lies Samoa. The Samoan ruler was a poor, no-account King with a salary of $20 a year and most of that was worked out by his subjects or came in the shape of store orders.

His navy was not much more formidable than a fleet of row boats.

So Kalakaua conceived the idea that Samoa would do well under Hawaiian rule, and forgot the great fact that what England might do with perfect propriety, being big enough, would in his case be considered a raw and bloody Bulgarian outrage.

It was given out that the royal navy of Hawaii was to be sent to Samoa to secure reciprocity. But I am informed that the reciprocity sought was of the kind which obtains in lion and lamb circles.

The little ship was fitted out with new paint and four 10-pounders. The king did not go himself, but he sent a number of officers, admirals, rear admirals, commodores, commanders, captains, some of whom had never been to sea before, to represent him.

Pinafore is called a comic opera, but beside this venture it would be as solemn as a mystery play of the middle ages.

The Royal Hawaiian Band of forty pieces, a really fine organization, also went along. There were carried more gin and whisky than coal, more gold lace than provisions.

The voyage to Apia is a long one, and before they got there the coal gave out. But they readily overcame this little difficulty by breaking up and burning the cases in which the gin came, and thus demonstrated the wisdom of bringing along so much juniper juice.

English, German, and American interests in Samoa made conquest hardly feasible, and the navy found that reciprocity wouldn't reciprocate. The mission was given up, but the band played some mighty fine music on the beach, and the officers paralyzed the barbaric Samoan court with its gold lace and female hats.

But the naval force had to eat. The poi got low in the barrel and the dried fish ran out.

One of the admirals had to chase around and see a grocery man. The Hawaiians wanted poi and salt horse on credit, but the dealer didn't take any stock in their promise to pay the bill on Saturday night. So they had to give security, and turned over the four 10-pounders, as being the things that could be spared most readily.

The Secrets of the Boudoir Exposed.

The idea of a blood-thirsty navy bent on war right away, without the means of even firing a salute, didn't seem to worry them.

So they got their poi and a little coal and some gin and turned the nose of the war ship homeward.

This trip so inured most of the officers to the kittenish ways of the fickle deep that they could go out in rather rough weather and not be sea-sick.

The Hawaiian navy is no more and its army is tired, so the government looks with complaisance at least on the presence of a representative of our navy, which is usually lying in Honolulu harbor.

Life on board the American ships, which looks as busy as a policeman's job, gets fearfully monotonous. But the bluff of being ready to fight before the other fellow can get off his coat shall and must be maintained.

So the officers have to act as though if they relaxed a little they would get hit by a half brick by the enemy. Life with the men is one hilarious round of scrubbing and painting, and scrubbing and scraping off the paint and scrubbing, and then painting again, month in and month out.

The boy who is contemplating running away and joining the navy had better make a note of this.

Every once in a while the officers give a ball. This, I suspect, keeps them from going crazy from the fearful dose of monotony and repeat. Burridge and I attended one of these balls.

It was a bright and joyous occasion, and Burridge will remember it a long, long time. On the evening of the festivities the Pacific was as calm and unruffled as an uncut custard pie. Off in the harbor lay the ship at anchor with the light against her rigging, giving it a phantom, cob-webby appearance against the blue sky of the tropical night.

The decks were draped in bunting above the rail, through which the light shone, colored and softened by the fabric, with an indescribably beautiful effect.

A steam tender and several of the ship's boats manned by sailors carried the guests off to the ship, and as we approached, music came floating over the water with all the added charm that distance and moonlight lends. The scene aboard was just as enchanting, with the grim engines of war masked by flags and smothered in flowers and festooned greenery. Populate the scene with four hundred people in evening

Take Off my Vest.

dress, the ladies with superb toilets, and one can imagine what our navy looks like when it dances with its friends.

A few days before when Burridge got his invitation, a realizing sense of the fact came over him that he was 5,000 miles away from his dress suit, and he was as sore as a stone bruise. Lieutenant Morrell, to whom he confided his canker, told him to come any way,—come in his overalls and no one would make any remarks.

But he gave it up until some one suggested

borrowing. He make known his great grief, and accommodating but lean friends came nobly to the rescue.

He borrowed a pair of trousers from Colonel Cobb. Mr. J. T. Ball, of Chicago, loaned him an evening coat which had been left in his custody by a friend who had gone down the islands.

He got a vest of a third gentleman who was fat. When it was put on it hung out like a parachute or a ballet dancer's skirt.

I may be doing wrong in divulging the secrets of the boudoir, but the truth has to go. I took in about a half bushel of slack in the vest and tied it up with twine.

Burridge kicked all the time and said he would't go. I really believed he couldn't have been kept at home by a broken leg. But I argued with him with a mouth full of pins, and I think I persuaded him that he looked like a bird—the breed not specified.

After we got aboard and became interested in the mazy dance and more mazy punch, Burridge commenced to forget himself.

It seems that he had made some solemn pledges to the owners of his clothes concerning the same. In relaxing his vigilance he commenced to smash the pledges like an independent candidate after election.

Carking care was seen on the collective brows of the syndicate of clothing owners.

Then they commenced to follow Burridge around in a body. He sat down to converse with a pretty girl. Colonel Cobb rushed up and called him aside.

"See here Burridge," he said, "you promised me not to sit down in those trousers. I don't want them if you' are going to get them baggy in the knees. Please remember your promise to me."

After a lively dance Burridge commenced to breath hard. This alarmed Mr. Ball, who sought him out.

"Mr. Burridge, that coat is a pretty tight fit, and if you persist in throwing your shoulders forward you will have it split up the back. It doesn't belong to me, and I want you to be more careful. You have let a lady deposit some face powder on the collar, too. I didn't think this of you."

The gentleman who loaned him the pumps reminded him pointedly just as he was asking a lady to dance that he had pledged himself not to trip the l. f. toe as long as he stood in the speaker's shoes.

The man who owned the vest was wild when he saw the result of my carpenter work on it.

"Take off that vest," he peremtorily demanded, "or let it out, I don't care which. I won't have it dragged out or shape."

No one could stand this, and Burridge feigned illness or insanity or something, and went below to the gun deck, where he sat and smoked cigarettes in the shadow of a big gun, using half breaths all the time. This is why I think he will remember the festivities a long time.

CHAPTER XIII

The Sweets of Loafing—The Land of To-morrow—Suspicious of Hustlers—A Man in a Mother Hubbard—The Mahopi Habit.

I HAVE always had a sort of sneaking regard for the conscientiously lazy man; he who has the strength of character to defy public opinion and to industriously devote himself to the sweets of indolence with the calm placidity of the truly great. Such a man is a king. He is more—he is a czar, and serenely entails suffering on others with the matter-of-course feeling which only belongs to absolute monarchs and pretty women.

Thoreau, whose chief glory was that he could wear a patch or even a sunbonnet without a blush, found by actual experiment that seventeen days of labor would keep a man a year even in grudging New England, and that the hustle of the remaining 348 days went only to buy food which did not agree with us, clothes which were for show not protection, and gilded shelter.

The Apostle of Simplicity worked hard and then he loafed hard. It always seemed to me that he was not only sane but sensible.

There are a good many men in America to whom the greatest compliment of life is to be called "hustlers." They tear around like village people at a fire for twelve or fourteen hours a day, six days in the week, and fret all day Sunday about business—for what? Simply, they will tell you, to make a pile before they die, so that they can retire from business and enjoy life.

Of course there are numbers with the magpie instinct who want to heap up a pile for the fun of the thing, so that they can sit on the chilly apex of the same with a shot gun and be envied by the equally misguided but less fortunate. But these are not the masses, and the mass is what I am talking about.

Most of them are struggling in the hope that some day they can live on their incomes and become

48

respectable loafers and raise fancy pups and go fishing six days in the week and even on Sunday, if they are quiet about it.

But this dream is of the future, and it seems better—more certain—to collect the bill for labor on the instalment plan and raise our pups and go fishing as we travel along.

And that is what threw me into a trance of admiration over the islands. It is fashionable to be lazy.

"Sit on the Chilly Apex."

There are hustlers there who build railroads and resort hotels and lay out town sites and sell lots and conduct themselves generally in the misguided Chicago fashion. But they are looked upon with suspicion.

The common way is to take life as easily as the head Indian fighter does in the border drama with his trusty rifle.

It's the climate, of course, that makes it so. When a tourist first comes he works ten hours per day at the sight-seeing trade. Then he joins himself in an eight-hour movement, which is invariably successful. This is rapidly decreased until he sits on the Hawaiian Hotel piazza and dreams and smokes for sixteen hours out of a possible sixteen, and tries to stifle a guilty conscience, sore over the fact that he isn't getting his money's worth of sights.

Then the climate gets in its perfect work. Even his conscience refuses to rise up and accuse him, and it soldiers the happy hours away with the abandon of utter debasement.

If a man wants quiet and rest and has any natural reluctance to go to jail, Honolulu is the next best place on earth to get it.

The islands are called, and rightfully called, the land of the Mahopi. Mahopi means to-morrow, next week, by and by, or never, according to the context and the intent of the speaker. Its most exact translation, however, is "by and by." If you ask a native to do anything for you and he says, "All right, I will, mahopi," it means that you had better hustle for it yourself.

It is a very handy word and it is worked pretty hard in the local vernacular. The natives live up to the mahopi idea with religious consistency.

The most energetic citizens of the United States are the newsboys, and the gulf between them and the Honolulu article is something unspannable even in fancy. The little Kanaka boy who sells the *Pacific Morning Advertiser* and the *Evening Bulletin*, came to the hotel and stood in a shadowy corner of the corridor with one bare foot on the other and just looked sorry about something. His eyes were big and black and he gazed with much pathos at the people who could read, but he didn't do anything else to sell his papers. Indeed he seemed to part from them with a pang. One day *The Bulletin* referred to me as "genial and accomplished." I wanted a number of copies to decorate with a frame of blue pencil marks and send to a lot of people—acquaintances of mine—who don't know how good or great a man is until they see it in the papers.

Business Hours in Chicago.

He only had three or four copies and I tried to buy them, but it was like a special sacrifice sale—only one article would be sold to each person.

He explained that if he sold out, his business would be gone. I told him that he might go back to the city circulator and get all the papers remaining from that day's run and I would buy them.

He said, "Mahopi," and I haven't seen him since, while hundreds of Illinois people will go down to their

graves and never know how genial and accomplished I
am when away from home.

Instances of the mahopi habit spring up at every
hand. We stepped into the hut of a native in the out-
skirts of the town for a glass of water.

We found the gentleman of the house at home.
He had evidently said "mahopi" to some one a few
days previously and was waiting for the affair to blow
over. He was seated in a rocking-chair attired in his
wife's Mother Hubbard.

He was an exceedingly dignified, white-haired old
gentleman and received us with courtly courtesy and a
warm handshake.

Business Hours in Mahopi-Land.

Thoreau himself couldn't have worn the Mother
Hubbard with more queenly grace.

He explained casually that his only pair of jean
trousers were being mended or laundried or something.

At any rate, his good wife had them temporarily,
while instead of going to bed or bumping around in a
coarse, ill-fitting, headless barrel suspended by galluses,
as is the custom in the States under similar stress of
circumstances, he donned his wife's extra gown and
wore it like a perfect lady.

Had there been no such thing as mahopi in this
country he would probably have owned as many suits
of clothes as a professional beauty.

Mahopiism reaches clear into the realm of nature.
Take for instance that superb type of industrial activity, the mosquito.

The natives of the jungles of New Jersey or the
swamps of Indiana are tireless. They work night and
day, regardless of the behests of the trade unions, as

long as the supply of raw material holds out or does
not build a smudge.

It would seem that they did the same here to the
superficial observer. But we were not superficial ob-
servers—at least Burridge was not. He studied ento-
mology every night. After crawling carefully under

The Reluctant Newsboy.

his mosquito canopy, kicking his heels wildly in the
air to scare away those who would crawl under the
canvas with him, he commenced his researches. Usually there was a flock of mosquitos purring away up in
the gable end of his gauze tent. Then his career as the
great human insecticide began. You have seen a base-

He Wore his Mother Hubbard with Queenly Dignity.

ball catcher working hard with a pitcher who delivers
very wild balls. Well, that was Burridge to a nicety.

There wasn't any mahopi about his action. One
night after bagging considerable game, he stopped to
examine and heft some of the best trophies.

"Look here, Jones," said he, "this one don't weigh as much by a quarter of a pound as those I killed this morning; just heft it once," and he tossed it over to me.

He was right, and we asked the hotel clerk about the discrepancy in weight of the game of the place. We were informed that it would try the energies of one mosquito too severely to be obliged to work all the time, so it was arranged that tourists are to be chewed by different gangs.

They work in two shifts, a night and a day shift. The day workers are large and gray, while, as Burridge discovered, those who burn the midnight electric light are smaller and are of a jet black color.

The night gang seems to put more bichloride of scratch into its injections, but both shifts do a rushing business in the Dwight treatment.

It is very amusing to see them when one set of hands replaces another. When the 6 o'clock whistle blows the day gang lays down its drills or stops its pumping works, as the case may be, wipes off its bills and leaves its job.

Then the little black fellows come right in and take up the work, which goes on without a hitch. This arrangement prevents premature breaking down, paresis and all those ills incident to overwork. Mahopi is a great institution.

A Shark Hunter.

A BANANA PLANTATION

CHAPTER XIV.

Tropical Fruits—Their General Lack of Ginger and Flavoring Extracts—Pomological Disappointments—Private Recipe for Making Bread Fruit.

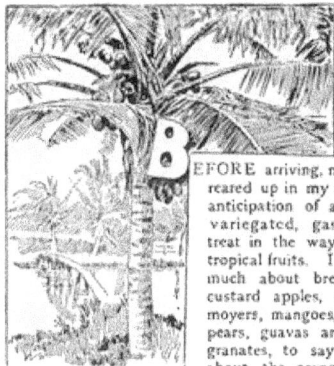

BEFORE arriving, my palate reared up in my mouth in anticipation of a radiant, variegated, gastronomic treat in the way of new tropical fruits. I heard so much about bread fruit, custard apples, or cherimoyers, mangoes, aligator pears, guavas and pomegranates, to say nothing about the oranges, bananas, cocoanuts and pineapples, that I made up my mind that I would order the whole pomological shooting match the first time I sat down at a table.

I was the victim of a cruel disappointment. When I reached that part of the Hawaiian Hotel's bill of fare, denominated by One Lung, the waiter, as " Flute," there were apples, imported from California; grapes imported from California; peaches, imported from California, and oranges, imported from California.

I did not like to kick about my food in public, for the man who does so is usually the one who lives on cotton batting baker's bread and fried liver when at home.

I didn't want the populace to think I had never eaten any fruit other than cucumber pickles and codfish balls, and so held my peace.

But I went out on a still hunt for anything that grew on trees and could be chewed by a determined man with sound teeth.

My first experience was with a fiery, untamed tamarind. It is an innocent looking product but it is loaded with vinegar.

I had eaten tamarind paste in the States which tasted like condensed lemonade, and was very good, so when Mr. Castle handed me a brown pod about as big as a man's thumb, and stood back to see me break out and talk anarchy, I thought his precaution unreasonable.

I tore open the shuck and found it contained a dark reddish mud in which were some hairs, that

52

looked as though the cook was a little careless, and two or three buttons. I culled out this debris and put the rest in my eager mouth.

It wasn't bad. It tasted like chemically pure tartaric acid toned down by lemon juice.

The Tamarind Effect.

My teeth curled up their toes and rocked on their foundations. I have been going around ever since with a mouth drawn up like that of an enthusiastic amateur flute player.

The name "breadfruit" is an attractive one and sounds toothsome. It had always been a youthful dream of mine to run away to sea and get wrecked on some balmy winter resort where I could go out and pluck my morning roll from the trees, and I still continued to cherish the dream when I found later in life that it was frequently necessary to get out of a cold winter night and hustle around with a pan of dough because Mrs. Jones had forgotten to set the "emptyns" near enough to the register.

But with all that, I am not willing to substitute breadfruit for bread without the fruit in the Jones family menu.

For the first two or three days at the hotel I stuck up my nose at biscuit, rolls, bread, flannel cakes and all that, and called hard at the Chinaman for breadfruit.

He invariably gave me the Chinese equivalent for the sentence, "I'm sorry, sir, but we are just out of breadfruit." That is, I suppose it was what he said. He may, however, have been calling me a thundering idiot. It is probably what he thought anyway.

I soon learned that if I was going to eat breadfruit I would have to be my own walking steward and possibly baker; so I started out to run down and corral a baking.

I first fell into the clutches of a low-down Chinese fruit vendor who sold me a citron, warranting it the finest kind of salt-rising breadfruit. I toted this shameless fraud around with me for two or three hours, until an acquintance casually asked me if I were going to make preserves.

After being set right I went back and hunted up the Chinaman who failed to recognize me. In fact, he said he never saw me before and that I had done my business previously with his twin brother, who was a disgrace to the family and had just been taken to jail.

He offered to sell me some taro root which was the genuine product of the flour and yeast tree, as he solemnly assured me on his yellow, slant eyed honor. But I had eaten taro and was angry. If I could have seen his dishonest brother it would have gone hard with one of us.

I chased around under a hot sun until I ran across a native with the real thing. They were green and had a surface like an osage orange, and were about the size of the smaller bowling-alley weapons.

I took it up to the hotel and told the steward that when it was light enough to go in the oven I wanted it cooked and served at our table. In two or three days,

Jones Plucking Bread.

or after it had ripened sufficiently, it was brought on.

It was not to be cut in slices, as one might suppose, but had to be broken open. I took a mouthful and stopped proceedings to diagnose the symptoms.

I believe that I hit it closer than a government assayer when I state that it was composed of 50 per cent sweet potato and 50 per cent fresh yellow beeswax. If any one wishes to know what baked breadfruit is like let him take those articles in the proportion named, mix them together carefully, and eat while hot, as the cook books say.

The most satisfying native fruits to be found are oranges, pineapples, and bananas, which are, of course, no novelties.

Pomegranates may also be found in the big cities of the States if one hunts for them, and it is easier to get one there than in Honolulu. As every one knows, they look like Ben Davis apples, with a sort of escape valve on the blow ends. They are divided into four compartments inside, each one being filled with cranberry sauce, in which is pretty thickly scattered loose passementerie trimming.

It takes patience to eat pomegranates, and I would pretty nearly as soon chew shoe pegs for sustenance.

Cocoanut palms are thicker than lamp-posts in America, but they have a way of growing high, and the nuts are hard to get. I was told that I must eat a green cocoanut on the half-shell if I wanted to enjoy life.

After serious difficulty we succeeded in getting a native to climb a tree and pluck some for us. They were cut open, and at the first one Burridge got wild because, as he said, we had been confidenced again. It contained nothing but some skimmed milk.

What he wanted was the good old United States cocoanut with celluloid insides. We cracked open another, and found after draining off the bilge water that it had just commenced to deposit celluloid.

This we dug out with a spoon, and found it was like eating the white of an egg, although it was a little smoother and tasted something like a slippery elm poultice.

Down on Hawaii we met a native with a bag full of custard apples or cherimoyers. He sold them three for a quarter and we invested heavily.

This fruit had been described as something unapproachable. It had been called vegetable ice-cream without the ice. I had begun to get suspicious, and made my custard apple exploration cautiously, but was rather agreeably surprised at its coming somewhere near the plans and specifications given out by enthusiastic travelers.

Still there is no occasion for excitement over it. Custard apples are very like our papaws with the strong Indiana flavor eliminated. When green they have a faint taste of turpentine, as do the mangoes.

The guavas are the fruit from which guava jelly is extracted. They grow on bushes that resemble the quince, have the external appearance of smooth lemons, and have an inside that looks like a miniature watermelon with a faint pink tinge before it is ripe. The flavor is sweet, faintly acid and faintly like cough medicine.

There are musk melons which grow on trees and are called paupuas, but they are not popular. The fact is, most tropical fruits lack flavor and point.

I tried everything in sight, from pumpkins to skoke berries, but failed to find anything which remotely approached strawberries at an ice-cream festival, or the old-fashioned watermelon by moonlight.

Natives preparing taro.

CHAPTER XV.

Dusky Sirens—Sentiment and Poi—Paradise Found at Last—No Change of Style for Fifty Years—The Last of the Mother Hubbard.

IN 1866 Mark Twain visited the Islands and described the female Kanaka's costume as a nightgown, which fit her like a circus tent does its center-pole. The center-pole has swelled since then, but the description answers just as well as it did twenty-five years ago. The dress, however, has acquired a name, although it is one which makes the American editor snort, paw the ground and shake his mane.

Just why editors in general and paragraphers in particular should foam at the mouth and conduct themselves in a way calculated to scare innocent children every time a Mother Hubbard is mentioned, is something I could never understand.

I am aware that they voice popular sentiment in this to a certain degree; and that a great many fool men go into cat fit delirium and revile the female sex because of its more or less secret passion for the Mother Hubbard.

In these days, when coat buttons have but feeble tenacity of purpose, and when apple pie has a damp basement crust with defective drainage, if I couldn't find a better excuse to abuse my wife than her morning Mother Hubbard debauch, I would shut up.

The garment is simple and effective and hangs more closely than any other in the lines of the classic raiment of ancient Greece and Rome, which is confessedly the esthetic garment in the whole range from fig leaves to plug hats and dress suits.

The Mother Hubbard is good enough for me. I don't mean that exactly, either. It might look strange in connection with my brand of whisker.

What I mean to say is that it is good enough for my female relations, if I am to be the umpire. I don't think it has ever had half a show in the States, although on the islands it has led the fashion for fifty years or more.

Its origin was one of necessity. The missionary mothers found, when it came to clothing the converts, that this style of gown was the simplest and easiest made.

When the Kanaka lady was aroused to the demands of polite society the missionaries were ready with a calico bag with a hole in the end for the head. These answered all the requirements, for the whites discreetly kept it dark that there were any such things as tailor-made suits.

Thus the Mother Hubbard became grounded in the affections of the saddle-colored populace, and there it has stuck ever since.

There are a number of solid people in Honolulu who have syndicated themselves together for the purpose of giving out the secret to the rest of the world that the islands are a paradise, and the only one which a great many of us will ever get a chance to see.

The Hawaiian Islands' other name is "Paradise of the Pacific."

Everybody thinks the place has a right to the name, because the air is softer than a love letter, and the showers come down as from a toy sprinkling-pot, and the moon is bigger, rounder, burns steadier and has more candle-power than that of any other company, and the sea-water is warmer than fresh-laid milk, and the ocean is bluer than a defeated candidate the day after election, and the scenery is more picturesque than a vision of jim-jams, and more grandly imposing than a State street policeman, and summer temperature

55

hangs at about 75 degrees on the average, and winter is only six degrees colder, and the people could not be more hospitable if you had your will made leaving them a million and was enjoying mighty poor health.

This is all true enough, but it isn't what makes the islands a paradise in my not particularly humble estimation.

Rah, or the Mother Hubbard!

To me this place is an infringement on the paradise patent only because the Mother Hubbard has full swing.

I am talking now to the fathers of grown-up daughters, present and prospective. Can anything in the masculine mind more closely approximate a place of sainted repose than this one, where there hasn't been a change of style for fifty years?

Just think of it! Young women can wear out their dresses if it takes two years.

No wild jump from one style to another every sixty days, or before a man has got the bills of the last style paid.

Hats the same way. With the masses—the female masses—small sailor hats of straw prevail, that can be worn alike winter and summer, and year in and year out.

Of course, there are exceptions. Some of the people send to the States or to Paris for their gowns, but they can afford it, and the change is not compulsory, as it is in America.

This island home of the Mother Hubbard is indeed a paradise.

Aside from their dress I was somewhat disappointed in the fair fat sex of the islands.

Beauty according to Caucasian standpoint, is rare among full blooded natives. Their eyes are big and black, with long lashes, but the other features are not pleasing, the lips being thick and the nose mashed down and running over into the cheeks.

But among the half whites one's admiration is liable to be called upon quite frequently. With noses and mouths derived from the white side of the house but retaining the fringed lashes and the lustrous ox eyes of the Kanaka branch, the resulting combination fits the picture more accurately as given out by travelers.

The hands of nearly all the females are so good that the like is rarely seen in the States, except on statuary. This is because they do little work and also

The Classic Mother Hubbard.

because, if my informant was correct, Kanaka mothers roll the fingers of their girl babies to make them taper, some times to the point of brutality.

We were riding on a railway train and I made a remark, overheard by the subject, on the wonderful beauty of the eyes and symmetry of the hands of one of the passengers.

After this the lady leaned over, put her hand up to her face, using her eyes as a Spanish woman might, in a way calculated to temporarily assuage my grief over the fact that Mrs. Jones was 5000 miles away.

Then she looked off into dreamy space in a manner that would make a poet shuck his coat and go to work getting out a new rhyme for "ambushed fire 'neath fringed lids," and to find a way to say something about "the midnight depths of the twin wells of her soul, measurable only by the plummet of human despair," and to say it gracefully and not as if the phrase had been dragged in by a pair of ice tongs.

I asked a friend what he supposed she was thinking about.

"Probably poi," he remarked, "and the superior taste of three over one-finger poi."

As I have intimated above, work dosn't seem to bother the fair sex. There isn't much to house-keeping, and the men do more of it than the women.

Poi is the staff of life. It is cheap and wholesome —also fattening.

It is made from the taro root, an esculent bulb about the size of a turnip, which grows in marshy places and has leaves very similar to water lilies. It is largely cultivated under irrigation.

Boiled or baked it comes on the table a dirty white, with the texture and some of the taste of yam, though flatter.

This root is peeled and usually powdered by hand in a large trough with a lava pestle, until the fiber is extracted and the coarse flour remains. This latter is moistened to the consistency of mush and is filed away for future reference.

When poi is wanted it is thinned to the consistency of paste and allowed to stand a day or two until it sours.

It is eaten by the fingers, the operator carefully taking his index finger, stirring it around in the bowl until a juicy gob is run down and captured.

It is then elevated to the mouth with a gentle spiral movement and tucked away with a swing very much like that an elephant uses when he throws confectionary into his hay-mow with his trunk.

After the second day, fermentation continuing, the poi becomes thinner and more sour, and it requires two fingers to carry the morsel safely to its destination. This is called "two-finger poi."

The poi continues to "work" like yeast—it is the only thing on the islands except Chinamen which does so—and by easy stages rises to the heights of three or four-finger poi.

This is the limit. Four-finger poi is put back to the one-finger grade by the addition of more mush.

It looks like sour paste, it smells like sour paste, and it tastes like sour paste. The appetite for it is usually acquired quickly and easily, and when one gets to be confirmed in the habit, there is nothing which will take its place.

It is usually eaten with a relish in the shape of salt-dried fish.

I became a shameless poi fiend, and can now understand the cockroaches' passion for the printing office paste-pot.

One can readily see that without any changes of fashion and with housekeeping consisting of seeing that the cover is on the poi keg when not in use, and attending to it that the codfish is hung up after each meal, the Kanaka housewife has lots of time to put flowers in her hair and struggle against her two hundred and fifty pounds of fat, in an effort to look romantic.

"Percentage of illiteracy small."

WASH DAY IN HAWAII

CHAPTER XVI.

Kanaka Character—Children of Sentiment—Peculiar Financial
Operations—Generous and Selfish at Once.

HE opportunities for
studying Kanaka char-
acter are not as plenti-
ful as some might sup-
pose, and while every
other person one meets
on the streets is a na-
tive, I was to a degree
disappointed in not get-
ting solidly acquainted
with the average abo-
rigine of the "Peaceful
Isles." The upper class
natives and half whites,
who, by the way, side in thought and feeling with the
coffee-colored fraction, and out-Kanaka the full-bloods

in their conflicts with adverse white influences, live as
do their most aristocratic white neighbors.

If anything, they are more punctilious and more
careful in social usages than the whites themselves.

That is, in public.

It is said that when they go in for comfort with
closed doors, they sit on the floor and eat raw fish and
poi with their fingers in the old way, for their liking for
poi, amounting to a passion, does not die with culture.

And just so far as they adopt the customs and con-
ventionalities of the whites they become uninteresting.

It is the masses of any nation that furnish anthro-
pologists food for thought and material for their pamph-
lets loaded with words so hard that an ignorant person
would take them for foul and abusive epithets.

I am no anthropologist, and may never do any an-
thropologizing to speak of, but I have more use for the
every-day barn-yard citizen with a hitch in his gait
caused by walking over plowed ground than I have for
the one who has just got out of the hands of a de-
corator and furnisher after being veneered and polished
with a lot of brand new culture and affectations.

So the Kanaka who has finished his or her education in Paris is less interesting to me than his humbler
brother, who has never been off the islands.

It is among the latter class that the old habits,
traditions, beliefs, and lines of thought are pursued.
As I said above one may see a great number without,
unless by special effort, becoming acquainted with them.

The house servants are Chinese, Japanese, and
Portuguese, the first predominating.

The Kanakas are a race of philosophers and have
a pardonable weakness for lying around in the shade.

Field labor is uninviting to native nature, and in this line they have been pretty generally supplanted by the smooth and oily Celestial.

They have no use for money except as a means of having a good time. The fear of a hungry to-morrow is not before them.

A Sentimental Native.

A day's labor will bring a week's poi, and poi with a little fish relish is all sufficient. The question of shelter need not worry any one, for a shack which affords as much protection as an American hen house, more than satisfies the average Kanaka.

The fuel problem does not exist. The first week or two we were there we wandered around looking at the houses with a strange haunting sense of something wrong—something wanting.

It was like eating bread with the salt left out. I couldn't exactly locate the deficiency. Burridge was troubled in the same way.

"Jones," said he one day, stopping in the street, "what is the matter with these houses. They don't look right."

"That's so, they don't." Then the light broke—I suddenly saw what it was. "I can tell what's the matter. They haven't got any chimneys. Its funny we never before noticed there are no chimneys in the place." Burridge was delighted to find out what had been fretting him, and he slept better that night after his mind was eased.

The item for clothing is a small one, a straw hat, a cotton shirt and jeans trowsers fitting out the male Kanaka, and a similar hat and mother-hubbard doing likewise for the female.

I purposely omit the mention of shoes and stockings for they are regarded more in the light of ornaments among the lower classes.

Bountiful nature having done so much in the way of pressing the button, the Kanaka finds it requires but little effort to do the rest.

One has to forgive him for his habits of indolence. I am not sure but that, under the circumstances, indolence is simply rare good sense.

An acquaintance with a Kanaka I have found is something which will stand cultivation.

He comes naturally by many traits which are accounted rare and exceptional virtues in older civilized communities—and also many that are not.

If one isn't too much steeped in utilitarian ideas he will come to like the natives immensely—as he likes children, or certain types of Southwestern whites who live for freedom—freedom from care, from work, from responsibility — the kind of freedom that Thoreau preached and tried to practice at Walden.

It is of course a mistake to measure the Kanaka by the standard of—say Chicago. If this is done he will in advance be found wanting, for he is a creature of sentiment.

A flower to him means more than a dollar, and a handshake more than bread.

A Financial Transaction.

The native wife may not have time to mend a rent in her mother-hubbard, but she can go out and pick flowers for a garland, sit in the shade for an hour to string them and deck herself like a queen, not because it is an anniversary or any special festial event but merely to present an attractive appearance as she goes down to the fish market to procure a half pound of squid.

The native fondness for flowers is as strong as a Chicago man's for money.

The rites of hospitality have a sacredness in the eyes of the Kanaka uncontaminated by living in Honolulu, which exist in few other places on earth.

The Honolulu native has come to be much like the rest of the world in this respect, but the old hospitable ways prevail in the more remote parts of the islands. This hospitality may mean bankruptcy for the host, but it goes if he takes a fancy to you.

He will massacre his only hog, assassinate his bunch of hens for your dinner, turn his family out of doors that you may have shelter, put himself, his wife, his sons and daughters, and his wife's relations at your disposal.

He will even hustle for you. The extension of his hospitality even goes to limits that can not well be spoken of.

On the other hand, if you are what is freely translated as "no good," you haven't money enough to buy a meal from him, unless he sees a chance of making you suffer. Then the transaction will take on all the appearance of revenge on the white race.

In financial matters the Kanaka is peculiar. If they are conducted on a basis of friendship one is loaded with an excess of good measure if not a gift outright, but if it is straight business your friend becomes as keen as an oriental and as cold as a chattel mortgage shark.

One day when we were ashore at a little landing on Hawaii, I picked up a primitive lamp cut out of lava in the refuse of a door-yard.

I asked the gentleman with me to buy it, as he spoke the native language.

He took me up to the hut and introduced me to the old lady who lived there. We shook hands and had a nice sociable talk without understanding anything each other said.

My friend then told her I was a good man and that I wanted her lamp which was no earthly good.

She very gladly gave it and was sorry she hand't another one to present me.

I caught sight of a gourd calabash with a nice color, which would make a good wall decoration. It was cracked and useless.

I proposed to buy it of her and started to negotiate for it, using an interpreter. This was business, and she modestly demanded $4 for it. The price of a good one in Honolulu is about 50 cents. Yet the lamp, which is one of the kind which is now only found in old graves, had a value of something between $15 and $25.

This incident is perfectly typical of native character.

The natives are no plodders, and there must be excitement in their work to keep them at it. This is one of the reasons they are such capable sailors, there being enough of variety and danger in it to make the calling interesting.

They are natural born politicians, having no principles to speak of and a deep-rooted yearning for a soft sitting job in the shade.

They seem to fill the lower grades of offices acceptably, but a lack of executive ability keeps the masses out of the best places. The Queen's cabinet was frequently white with a sprinkling of half-whites. But the pure-blooded native shines as a policeman or a small clerk. There were about sixty of the former in Honolulu, although the chief and captains are whites born on the islands.

Occasionally one sees a Kanaka behind a counter, usually as a clerk. The law seems to have attractions for those who rise above manual labor.

This profession is the stepping stone to a political career, and besides it affords an unlimited scope for speech-making, something dear to the native heart. Native lawyers are not uncommon, but they are rarely entrusted with important cases.

The educational system is one of high standing and the percentage of illiteracy is very small, nearly every native being able to read and write in his own language.

They are brave in their own way.

There have been but few tests of military pluck, and while they have not the dash in battle that Americans have in desperate situations or the dogged persistency of the British against odds, yet they will fight with vigor on accasions.

In the olden times it was the sport of Hawaii kings to go shark killing. A catamaran was prepared with a large bowl of chopped chunks of executed criminals or enemies for bait.

The boat was put to sea and the flesh was punched overboard through a hole in the bottom of the bowl.

This in a short time attracted all the sharks in the vicinity. When they became thick as fleas it was the custom of the chiefs and kings to dive into the school and coming up under the monstrous sea wolves stab one as they swam to the surface.

This may be great sport, but it would require more nerve than the average white man possesses.

It was the correct way of spending an afternoon for a Kanaka king, but as for me, give me lawn tennis.

The achievements of some of the divers of the present day attest the fact that the old shark-hunting spirit is not entirely extinct.

It is a pretty well advertised fact that the race is dying out.

It is estimated that there were about 400,000 inhabitants when Cook discovered the islands, a little over a hundred years ago. Superintendent of Census Rodgers report places the native population in 1891 at about 40,000, showing a decrease of 25 per cent in the last ten years. The causes for this form a more suitable subject for a medical treatise than a chapter of a descriptive work.

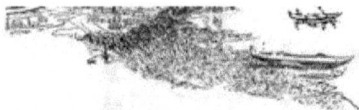

CHAPTER XVII.

A Smuggler Bold and the Custom House Russians.—The Pangs of an Amature in Crime.—War against the United States.

EFORE High Heaven I am inn-o-cent!"

I used this impassioned, fourth-act language, with the accent on the "o," in addressing the United States Government the day we landed in San Francisco. The hour was 9 a. m. The place was the Oceanic steamship dock in that city. The situation which wrested from me the above leading emotional appeal was due to my being constructively charged with smuggling—not actually in words, but by acts of pantomine and brutal conduct.

We had been aroused by the birth steward of the good ship Australia that day in the gray of the morning to see the sun rise over the highest priced real estate on the Pacific slope.

The air was chilly, but most of the passengers stood on deck watching the eastern purples turn to bronze, and the bronze to orange, and the orange back to the grays and browns of the forbidding coast as the sun came up and we neared the Golden Gate.

Many of the lady passengers grew sentimental at the sight of the United States colors, for they had been eating their ham and eggs for months under the hybrid

crazy quilt which did its work as the national flag of Hawaii.

I think we all had a feeling of relief at once more getting back to a land where we could josh royalty with impunity—a land where an ace outranks a queen every time.

I refer to this patriotic feeling because it really made our subsequent reception more painful.

As we steamed slowly up the bay the customhouse minions overhauled us and climbed over the rail with their pockets bulging with documents.

This reminded us that we would have to do some careless off-hand swearing, and possibly be required to expose the inside works of a grip-sack or two to the vulger official gaze, but we did not anticipate any Spanish inquisition business, or Russian convict treatment.

We had forgotten that Honolulu was the hot-bed of opium smuggling, but it seemed that the customhouse officers had not.

There was some fluttering among the passengers, especially those who had never before been out of the county, when the black whiskered custom-house keeper made us stand in line and gave us to understand that we musn't trifle with the United States.

I suddenly remembered that I had bought a Chinese fiddle, some trinkets and a new hairbrush in Honolulu, and I commenced to feel as sneaking as that time way back in 1879 when I swindled the government out of a dog tax by hiding him in the range oven.

He whined all the time I was talking to the assessor while I adroitly led the conversation away from the burning dog question.

But the man who keeps the custom-house didn't say anything about the Chinese fiddles and souvenir spoons and hair brushes, and I was too polite to introduce such painful subjects. I thought I caught him

61

looking suspiciously once or twice at my well-trained locks, and my heart throbbed, but he must have thought it was the engine if he heard it.

He asked me a lot of fool questions about my age, color, sex, previous condition of servitude, occupation,

Evading the Assessor.

pulse, temperature, respiration, appetite for spirituous or intoxicating liquors, what my grandparents died of, and if living why are they doing so, and a number of other things that I fail to remember. Then I was told to stand up and swear to it.

I arose, and he pronounced a hoodoo on me, stating, as near as I can remember, " Do-you-Strangulation-Jones-solemnly-swear-tum-te-tiddle-de-tum—with—malice-aforethought-onery-towery-tickery-tee-the-goods-chattels-merchandise-dickery-dickery-dock-except-as-herein-set-forth-alibo-crackibo-tender-lee-to-the-best-of-your-knowledge-and-belief-s'elpyou."

I told him I thought so and he let me go after I had signed my name.

That seemed easy and I went back to the state-room and planted the fiddle and souvenir spoons deeper down in my gripsack to avoid mistakes.

I confess that I began to have a feeling of vague unrest and wondered a little how they punished the Chinese fiddle and souvenir spoon brand of perjury in California.

I even considered the advisability of going to the custom-house man and confessing to the spoons and the fiddle and filing an application with the government for all the mercy it had on hand.

I talked with Burridge about it, and he said we should bluff the United States or bribe the officials.

He thought if I gave up the fiddle, spoons and hairbrush, and $10 in cash it would be all right. I kept getting more and more uneasy in my mind, and went on deck, where an old traveler who had been through the custom-house numerous times told horrible stories of the confiscation of property, and mentioned jewelry and silverware as being just what the officers were delighted to seize.

I excused myself, went below, and dug out the spoons, depositing them in my coat-tail pockets.

After that I had to walk around with great care

for fear of bumping against something and being betrayed by the clank of the silver.

Sitting down was out of the question. I commenced to realize that the criminal's lot is not a happy one. Although the day was cold my brow was beaded with perspiration. I firmly resolved if ever I got the spoons and the fiddle to Chicago, I would retire from the crime business and reform.

All this time the Australia was nearing the wharf. It was finally warped in and the gang-plank stuck out.

Then all those male passengers who had wives or sweethearts on hand to receive them, and those lady passengers who had husbands or young men there rushed together and clinched in a very vigorous manner.

I managed to walk down the plank gingerly, yet with a certain dignity with my guilty coat tails dangling heavily behind. A steward followed with the grip containing the contraband fiddle.

We were met by a line of men armed with chunks of chalk.

I felt that the critical moment had arrived and opened the grip with as much of an appearance of innocence as a man steeped in crime can assume on fair notice.

The inspector, who I was sure could see that fiddle through several strata of old clothes, paper novels and democratic lines, merely bent down and chalked some marks on the grip while he watched a pretty girl dicker with a hack man.

" Is that all?" I asked.

"That's all, unless you have something in the baggage-room."

The "Courier for the Czar."

I nearly fainted with joy at getting through and swindling the government out of a dollar and a quarter. To be sure we had five boxes in the steamer's baggage-room, but they only contained artists materials, Buridge's sketches of the volcano of Kilauea, lava from the same, and a lot of truck on which there was no commercial value and therefore not dutiable.

We told the inspector we would take the boxes at once to avoid a trip to the wharf again.

A change flashed over his countenance.

He saw in us a pair of desperate opium smugglers. Moreover, a new light dawned on us. We thought we had reached a place called United States, but were mistaken. It was Russia.

We mildly preferred a request to have the boxes. "Youse will not getivitch thim-off to-day-ivitch. Dey has got to be examined-off."

"Clinched."

"Can't you examine them now?"

"Oi dunno Av youse git somewan t' open de boxesivitch an' putoff upivitch fur it p-r-raps yonse kin," remarked the custom-house boyer carelessly. "Oi hov a mon ferninst-ivitch t' office what wu'l do yure wurruk chape-off."

The man "ferninst de office" came up, and we saw that he was armed with an obtuse ax and a crowbar which had curviture of the spine.

We hired him for $2 to open the boxes.

The ax and crowbar maestro turned a box up on edge and played an obligato in G minor on it with his weapons, while Burridge danced in the background.

The man with the ax had the instincts of a burglar but not the qualifying experience.

No artist can see his work pried out of a mess of debris with a crowbar without suffering the pangs of vivisection.

But when the despots dragged out one of Burridge's volcano sketches which were as red as the floor where a murder has been committed, the whole crowd was paralyzed with admiration.

"Whooroo, but they'r illigent," exclaimed one of the Slavs.

"That's what." assented another who seemed to have an idea that he was the Czar's understudy.

"They'er just as foine as a fortygraf," commented the head boyer, "an' they'r worruks of airt, an' as such are jutyable. Saze thim."

Burridge was in a spasm of apprehension and protested that he was an American citizen, had bought his painting material in Chicago and had a right under the law to bring in the county studies and sketches made abroad.

The head Russian stopped him early. "I belave you'r a loir, sor, and I belave you'r furriners and you'r so crazy anxius about thim boxes that I woulden't fall dead av we wuz to diskivver opeum in them. They are sazed in the name of the law. Youse otter be ashamed av yersilves comin' to our country an' thryin' to desave de gover'mint wid yer ile painted kromos."

It was in vain we protested that our fore-fathers fought and bled and died at Bunker Hill. The only response we got was in choicest Russian. The inspector merely answered in witty Slav repartee, "Aw, wot's 'atin youse."

We were led away in a nearly fainting condition and clambered aboard a telega, as George Kennan says, and directed the driver to take us to the Occidental etape.

Here Burridge started in to drown his grief in vodka. We were advised by sympathetic friends to hire a custom-house solicitor, fee him well, and declare war on the United States.

We did this, of course. Hostilities commenced by our going down to the custom-house and swearing to nine different documents at once. I didn't know exactly what it was for, but I expected it was to bring trouble to some one very soon.

Then we had to chase around and see people who had influence with the czar of the custom-house who finally granted us an audience after a dozen or so trips. We told him we wanted to get Mr. Burridge's paintings and my chunks of lava out of the clutches of the government as soon as possible.

He wanted to know what else we had in the boxes.

I frankly told him that there was nothing except a pair of old trousers that Mrs. Jones would want to cut down for Jones, Jr., and I couldn't see what use the United States had for them.

I also freely explained how all the dutiable goods I had brought in had been easily smuggled through on the day of my arrival, and those which remained were entitled to entry free of duty, and we wanted them right away.

He was very kind with his mouth, and promised it should be attended to at once. But it wasn't. We stayed with him several days before we got the goods, swearing to some new document every few minutes before a notary during business hours and without the assistance of a notary after business hours. We finally found out what was the matter. Had we been really genuine opium smugglers we would have got through long before. They are the only people who have no trouble with the officials.

FINIS.